Illustrated BUYER'S ★ GUIDE™

GTO

D1396660

Paul Zazarine

MBI Publishing Company

First published in 1994 by MBI Publishing Company, PO Box 1, 729 Prospect Avenue, Osceola, WI 54020-0001 USA

The information in this book is true and complete to the best of our knowledge. All recommendations are made without any guarantee on the part of the author or Publisher, who also disclaim any liability incurred in connection with the use of this data or specific details.

We recognize that some words, model names and designations, for example, mentioned herein are the property of the trademark holder. We use them for identification purposes only. This is not an official publication.

MBI Publishing Company books are also available at discounts in bulk quantity for industrial or sales-promotional use. For details write to Special Sales Manager at Motorbooks International Wholesalers & Distributors, 729 Prospect Avenue, PO Box 1, Osceola, WI 54020-0001 USA.

Library of Congress Cataloging-in-Publication Data

Zazarine, Paul.
    Illustrated GTO buyer's guide / Paul Zazarine
        p. cm. — (MBI Publishing Company illustrated buyer's guide series)
    Includes index.
    ISBN 0-87938-839-0
    1. GTO automobile–Purchasing. 2. GTO automobile—Collectors and collecting. 3. GTO automobile—History. I. Title. II. Series.
    TL215.G79Z394   1994
    629.222'2—dc20   93-32134

On the front cover: The 1967 GTO convertible with the 335hp 400ci engine owned by Linda Rutt of Palm Bay, Florida. *Mike Mueller*

Printed in the United States of America

Contents

Acknowledgments

This book is not the first I have written about the Pontiac GTO, nor, hopefully, will it be the last. Over the last seventeen years, I have had the opportunity to build some strong friendships thanks to owning and writing about GTOs. I have learned much about these great cars by talking to the people who created them. I have also learned much from the people who revere them today. They lovingly restore the GTO, research its history and, by immersing themselves in the car and the muscle-car culture it created, perpetuate the GTO legacy for generations to come.

I have had the pleasure of photographing hundreds of GTOs, and many of them are in this book. It is impossible for me to thank each of the owners here. All I can say is if you recognize your GTO in these pages, please accept my thanks once again for allowing me the honor of photographing it.

There are some people whose passion for the GTO and the GTO hobby inspires me. Chuck Roberts of Laurel, Maryland, taught me to appreciate the GTO as a unique performance automobile. His idea of combining the best parts from other GTOs to enhance the performance of his 1965 GTO led me to coin the phrase "restification" in the early 1980s. Chuck's GTO appears virtually stock from the outside, but inside and underneath it is chock full of modifications from other years. His trademark was installing a set of Grand Prix parking lights in the grilles. They look so good I wonder why the factory never thought of it.

Bill Schultz is well known for his Royal Bobcat 1969 Ram Air V GTO. Bill has researched the Royal story and probably knows more about this famous Pontiac dealership than anyone else (aside from Jim Wangers!). One room of his house in Warren, Michigan, is devoted to the GTO and to Royal. It's practically a museum, full of promos, literature, and other collectibles. I can't think of anyone more anxious to share knowledge about Royal and the GTO than Bill.

I've been involved in one way or another with the GTO Association of America since 1982, first as newsletter editor, PR flack, and "idea guy." For five years, the demands of editing magazines stole all of my time, but in the past few years I have again become involved, thanks to the efforts of Eric White. Eric became president of the GTOAA at a time when the club was in utter chaos. Under his guidance, a lot of fences were mended, and thanks to his calming presence and commitment to the car and the club, the GTOAA is once again growing and returning to its original premise as an organization dedicated to serving the GTO enthusiast. I highly recommend joining the GTOAA. For more information, write it at 1634 Briarson Drive, Saginaw, MI 48603.

If you own an IBM or compatible computer, I recommended purchasing Tygersoft's GTO Software. It is a comprehensive listing of GTO codes and other information about all years of production, and includes engines, transmissions, intakes, carburetors, batteries, and lots of other coded and part number information. It also allows the user to punch in information to identify the car or parts he or she has. Much of the production, color codes, and other information was used here, with permission, from Tygersoft. It's well worth the $39.95 (plus $3.95 shipping and handling). There's even a money-back guarantee if you don't like it. GTO clubs can order several at a discount. To order, contact Tygersoft at P.O. Box 1222, Vernal, UT 84078.

To track GTO prices for the last fifteen years, Eric Lawrence at CPI Value Guide was kind enough to assemble the charts that appear in each chapter. The CPI Value Guide is a quarterly price guide that tracks values for all collector cars, and the listings are always on the nose. It can also provide a historical price analysis that tracks the value of your specific GTO for the past ten years. A yearly subscription costs $20 and includes four quarterly issues. For more information or to order a subscription, contact CPI Value Guide, P.O. Box 3190, Laurel, MD 20709.

Finally, my thanks to Fred Simmonds at Pontiac Motor Division, Jim Mattison at Pontiac Historical Services, Donald Farr at Dobbs Publications, and especially to my parents, Sal and Ellen Zazarine. Their love and support has never wavered, no matter how many twists the road of life has taken for us all.

Introduction

It's the general consensus among collector car hobbyists that the Pontiac GTO was the first musclecar. Before the GTO arrived, high performance was restricted to expensive cars such as the Corvette, the Chrysler 300 series, or special order lightweight coupes like the Super Duty Catalina or the Z11 Chevrolet. When Pontiac boldly chose to drop the big Bonneville 389 engine into the restyled 1964 Le Mans midsize body, it delivered a new definition of automotive high performance and rewrote the history books.

In the eleven years—from 1964 to 1974—that the GTO roamed the boulevards, it created an aura of affordable performance that was also a rolling statement about the owner. The GTO literally ruled the streets in 1964 and 1965—nothing could touch it for under $3,000. By 1968, Pontiac's competitors had caught on and caught up, building cars that were faster and in some cases, less expensive. Still, before the bottom fell out of the market in 1971 due to a consorted effort on the part of the insurance industry, the GTO was the best-selling of the musclecar genre. When the ax fell at the end of the 1974 model year, Pontiac had built and sold over 500,000 GTOs. No other musclecar series built before 1974 ever came close to that kind of volume.

During the 1973–1974 Arab oil embargo, the price of gasoline skyrocketed and the value of musclecars (GTOs included) plummeted. They were labeled "gas guzzlers" as the emphasis shifted from performance to fuel economy. Although the GTO followed the normal depreciation cycle of all used cars, its depreciation was accelerated somewhat by the public's rejection of big-engined cars that could only run on expensive high-test gas and delivered poor fuel economy.

While these falling prices hurt the GTO's standing in the used car market, it was a boon to young performance addicts who found the GTO to be very affordable. By 1975, solid examples with the top performance options were selling for less than $1,000. Few examples remained stock with factory equipment intact; most GTOs that fell into young and hungry hands in the seventies suffered the ravages of modification. Interiors were scuttled, instrument panels were cut up to accept aftermarket gauges and radios, and factory induction systems were trashed to be replaced by aftermarket intake manifolds and carburetors. Along the way wiring systems were butchered, factory road wheels were replaced with "mags," and rear suspensions had their geometries revised, often to the severe detriment of front suspension components.

The first wave of serious collectors (who were ahead of their time in predicting the emergence of the musclecar as collectible) entered the GTO market in the mid-1970s while the prices were reasonable and some cars had escaped the hands of the street racers. Collectors who attempted to restore GTOs encountered some problems. Although plenty of parts were still available from Pontiac and prices were reasonable, those items that had been slashed from the parts books, like soft trim, were virtually impossible to find. Restorers had to improvise, and it was not unusual to find an incorrect trunk mat or J. C.Whitney dash applique installed in restored GTOs, simply because originals or exact reproductions didn't exist.

Also in the late seventies and early eighties, the definition of a GTO restoration included adding options or changing drivetrains, and within the GTO community this practice was perfectly acceptable. A four-barrel 389 with automatic transmission and 3.23:1 open rear could easily be converted to a Tri-Power four-speed car with 3.90:1 gears, thanks to a junked donor GTO, an engine hoist, and a few weekends of work. All of the parts were correct for that particular year vintage and had been installed as the factory would have done. While engine codes were correct, restorers were not sophisticated enough to understand date codes on heads, blocks, transmissions, and rear axles. As long as it looked "factory," it was absolutely acceptable. In fact, owners would oftentimes boast about how many options their GTOs now sported. The pastime of pasting on options soon overshadowed the fact that most original GTOs weren't loaded down with enough options to shame a Grand Prix!

This practice of overloading came back to haunt those owners in the late eighties, as restorers became knowledgeable about date codes and how they correlated to body build dates. GTO (as well as other Pontiac) owners also have the luxury of a service that few other Detroit automakers supply: Pontiac will authenticate the car by supplying a copy of the original billing invoice. The billing invoice provides the VIN number and a listing of the factory-installed options. This eliminates the possibility of buying a faked GTO or GTO Judge. Documentation is the best way of verifying a GTO's "pedigree" and has saved many buyers the agony of purchasing a counterfeit GTO.

Documentation

If you are contemplating the purchase of a GTO, Judge, or other Pontiac, it is highly recommended that you send the VIN (vehicle information number) and a check for $25 to Pontiac Historical Services, Attn: Jim Mattison, P.O. Box 884, Sterling Heights, MI 48311-0884. You will receive a packet of information about your model year along with a copy of the billing invoice. This invoice contains the VIN and the options as installed by the factory. It will help you avoid purchasing a counterfeit GTO or Judge and will authenticate the pedigree of your GTO.

Chapter 1

Buying a GTO

Market History

The collector car market exploded in 1987 after the collapse of the stock market. Investors, who had been burned by paper stocks, began putting their money in tangibles. Some invested in art, others in coins, antiques, and other valuables. Younger investors turned to cars, mostly postwar cars like Corvettes, 1957 Chevrolets, and Shelby Mustangs, and the value of these cars went ballistic. Those 1967

Some very special GTOs have been built over the years. Among the most famous are the 1964–1969 Royal Bobcats. They were sold by a small Pontiac dealer in Royal Oak, Michigan. For additional cost, Royal would perform modifications like engine swaps (389 to 421 or 400 to 428) as well as engine hop-ups, suspension work, and other performance enhancements. These cars are extremely rare and quite valuable. Since Royal got out of the performance car business in 1969 and no records survive from the dealership, documenting a Royal Bobcat is virtually impossible unless genuine paperwork appears with the car. The two 1966 Gee-TO Tigers shown here were specially prepared and drag raced at exhibitions across the United States. *Courtesy Jim Wangers*

Corvettes equipped with the L71, L88, or L89 engines broke the $100,000 mark, while Shelby Mustangs commanded even more. Musclecars also became the darlings of the investors/collectors, especially rare models like Hemi 'Cudas and LS6 Chevelles. At the height of the frenzy, some of these cars changed hands for more than $150,000. These cars were the most powerful of their breed, and thanks to low production numbers (only seven 1971 Hemi 'Cuda convertibles were produced, for example), the demand was high, pushing their prices up to astronomical levels in a short period of time.

While this price spiral was great for speculators who bought early and sold high, it also benefited the hobbyists who had owned their cars for a number of years and profited immensely by selling while the market was strong. For those who had no portfolio and

The GTO's origins can be traced to the 1961 Tempest, a unit-bodied car with four-cylinder engine (actually a 389ci V-8 "sawed" in half), flexible drive shaft, rear-mounted transaxle, and independent rear suspension. The words "performance" and "Tempest" weren't used in the same sentence in 1961.

By 1963, the Tempest series had been upgraded and restyled, and the troublesome independent rear suspension redesigned. The Le Mans model had been added, providing a more sporty flavor to the dowdy Tempest. A 326ci V-8 was added for more pep. Better things were to come in 1964.

In 1964, Pontiac redesigned the Tempest series and abandoned the "half a V-8" engine, as well as the unit body, rope drive shaft, rear transaxle, and unit body. Two series were offered: the base Tempest and the Le Mans. The Le Mans had a new performance option called GTO.

From 1964 to 1973, the midsize Tempest, Le Mans, and GTO series used a separate body and frame. The body was mounted to the frame on fourteen rubber bushings. The radiator core support was mounted to two front bushings for a total of sixteen mounting points. The front sheet metal attached to the radiator support and to the cowl of the body shell. In 1974, the GTO was an option on the Ventura, a unit body derivative of the Chevy Nova.

wanted to get into the musclecar hobby, either to invest or participate as a hobbyist, it was virtually impossible to buy the cream of the musclecar crop. At one point during the madness of 1989–1990, overseas buyers were walking around at shows with briefcases crammed with money, ready to buy cars and take them out of the country.

Just like most investments built on speculation, the bottom fell out in 1991 when the recession struck hard. For those who got out before the prices plummeted, the losses weren't as bad. But for those who had paid $120,000 for a 1967 L71 Corvette, it was a hard financial blow, because by the spring of 1992, that same Corvette wasn't even pulling $50,000 at auctions.

While the Corvettes, LS6 Chevelles, and Hemi Mopars were on the front lines of the investment wars, musclecars like the GTO were enjoying their own value appreciation, although not at the dizzying rate of the high-demand cars. Instead, the GTO's appreciation was like an inclined plane, steady at about 5 to 10 percent per year. Some models such as the 1969–1970 Ram Air IV and 1964–1966 Tri-Power convertible appreciated somewhat faster. But, for the most part, America's first musclecar was not the first choice of collectors. For the GTO hobbyist, that proved to be good news because as the musclecar market collapsed under the weight of investors and speculators, GTO prices didn't fall as hard or as far. Consequently, for the true hobbyist, the Pontiac GTO remains one of the best buys on the market today.

Making the Right Choice

For those looking to buy a GTO (or any collector car, for that matter), the first rule to remember is not to buy over your head, and that means not just from a financial investment standpoint. Factor in how much time and work will be required to restore the car. If you've handled extensive restorations before, then you are familiar with the necessary procedures, tools, equipment, shop space, parts chasing, and restoration that are necessary. You should be familiar with what you are capable of doing and what you have to farm out to experts. Few of us can reupholster seats or do body and paint work like an expert. Send-

ing this work out will ensure quality work (however, not all shops are reputable—do your homework first!), but it will also cost you more.

If you aren't capable of performing a restoration yourself, but have the means to buy a rare GTO and have it restored, make sure the restoration shop is knowledgeable about GTOs and can do the proper job. The costs here can be astounding. Assume you buy a 1965 GTO convertible loaded with the optional Tri-Power engine, four-speed gearbox, air conditioning, and other desirable accessories, but it's in rough shape. You pay perhaps $5,000 for a complete numbers-matching car, then take it to a restoration shop and pay upwards of $20,000 (or more) for the restoration. If you're lucky, you may break even. The GTO market has a hard time supporting cars over the $25,000 mark, so it may take some time before you have any equity. If investment isn't a consideration, then the point is moot. If you want to make some money in the long run, consider the initial cost of purchase plus the cost of restoration. If the equation gives you negative equity and that is a prime consideration, you might want to rethink your strategy.

If all you want to do is wax the fenders of a pristine original or a correctly restored model that requires no work, be prepared to pay top dollar. Don't shop for bargains because you should consider condition before price. Obviously you want the best car for the best price. But looking for bargains can work against a buyer. Be suspicious of high-demand cars with low prices, because there's a wolf in the hen house. Ask some hard questions such as, how much work was done on the car and who did the work, and examine the date codes and other information closely.

It's essential that you are familiar with these codes and dates. Several years ago a dentist purchased at auction what he thought was a 1965 GTO convertible. It was red and was equipped with Tri-Power and four-speed, and his winning bid was $20,000. Not long after purchasing the car, he entered it in a Pontiac show. The judges there advised him the car was equipped with the wrong engine and a 1966 Tri-Power setup, had an incorrect transmission, and had a 1964 Le Mans interior

The 1964–1973 perimeter design frame consisted of two fixed crossmembers and a bolt-in member to support the transmission. The frames used torque boxes for added stiffness, but 1964–1971 convertible models featured a boxed frame for additional rigidity. This boxed frame was optional on hardtops and coupes for several years. The most trouble-prone areas for rust are at the rear crossmember at the coil spring mounting points.

as well. Failing to do his homework cost him at least $15,000.

Matching Numbers

One of the most popular terms in the collector car hobby is "the numbers match." What that means is simply that all the production dates are in line with the build date of the vehicle. For example, assume you are looking at a 1966 GTO with a build date of 10C (this information is found on the data plate located on the left hand side of the firewall). The first two characters denote the month of assembly (10 = October). The last character indicates the week of the month (C= third week). You now know the car was an early production, built the third week of October 1965. A low serial number will also bear this out.

To ensure that the engine block, heads, intake and exhaust manifolds, transmission, rear axle, and other components are correct, their date codes must be earlier than the build date of the car. Casting date codes begin with a letter (A=January, B=February, and so on) followed by two digits representing the date

of the month, which is followed by a third digit representing the year the component was cast. For example, a head cast on March 17, 1967, would read C 17 7.

Engine blocks are both coded and dated. The coded information, which appears on a machined pad on the left-hand front of the block, denotes the engine application. For example, a 1966 GTO manual-transmission-equipped car would have a WS code, while an automatic car would read YS. Beneath these codes is an engine serial number that was independent of the vehicle identification number until 1968, when federal law required the last eight digits of the VIN be used as the engine serial number as well. The engine also has a casting date next to the distributor hole at the top rear of the block. This is important to note, since a few block codes were recycled in later years, and Pontiac blocks, from the 326 right up to the 455, all share the same exterior dimensions. For information regarding engine codes and casting dates, consult the GTO Restoration Guide, available from Classic Motorbooks.

Buying a GTO

Which year GTO should you buy? That question can be answered objectively if investment is the motivating factor, because

The GTO Association of America, one of the largest supporting organizations for the GTO, holds organized events across the country, including the yearly national convention. This national event was held at the Indianapolis Motor Speedway and one of the activities was a few laps around the legendary Brickyard.

there are some gold-plated years and models to look for. Any convertible from 1964–1971 is a good investment. So is a car equipped with the top performance engine. Some GTOs were decked out with more options than a Bonneville, but beware, because some of those options may have been added when the car was restored. To some in the GTO hobby, these additions enhance the value of the car only as long was they are correctly installed. Others may balk at a car whose options don't match up with the billing invoice.

The 1969 GTO Judge is anther desirable model. Its low production and unique status make it an excellent choice, and you can stack more desirability onto it by purchasing a Judge convertible with the top-performance engine. Choosing which GTO to buy can also be a subjective decision based on the buyer's desires. If you and your spouse-to-be started dating in high school, and you drove a 1973 GTO, your desire to again own a 1973 GTO is purely sentimental. There's nothing at all wrong with buying a 1973 for that reason, but don't be disappointed when you have a tough time trying to pedal your 1973 GTO in the collector car market because it isn't a high-demand model. Be aware of the ramifications of your purchase before you buy.

Modified cars on the whole are a poor investment. A customized 1969 hardtop with a trick paint job, lots of chrome, and a blower poking out of the hood may look good in Car Craft, but you will never recover the money invested to build up the car. A mild restification is much easier to handle, since you can unbolt the incorrect parts and replace them with originals before selling the car. In the GTO field, correctness adds significantly to the value of the vehicle.

Catching a Counterfeit

It's especially important to take great care when contemplating the purchase of a GTO. Not only should you be concerned about rust, body and frame damage, and incorrect drivetrains and accessories, you should consider the danger of buying a counterfeit GTO.

In 1964 and 1965, the GTO was an option on the Le Mans series. Consequently, it bears the series number for the Le Mans, and there is no way of identifying a GTO from the VIN. While there have been some attempts at verifying a 1964–1965 GTO's authenticity through codes on the firewall data plate, it is still an

Here's an enigma wrapped in a mystery. Is this a 1965 GTO or not? The tip-off is the trim panel between the taillamps. The GTO's taillamps have a six-rib design that carries across the center trim panel. Tempest and Le Mans have a ten-rib design. This car has GTO taillamps and a Le Mans center trim panel. Is the car a Le Mans converted to a GTO by a counterfeiter who didn't have the correct trim panel? Or is it a GTO whose owner incorrectly replaced the panel? Only the billing invoice, which shows the VIN and the options, will reveal the truth. These are the types of clues you'll have to decipher as you search for the perfect GTO.

GTO shows are held across the country, bringing cars, owners, and vendors together. They provide great opportunities for looking over restored GTOs, talking to owners, purchasing literature and parts, and checking out the GTO corral to see what's for sale.

imperfect science, since some documented GTOs have no coding information on the firewall at all.

From 1966 until 1971, the GTO was assigned its own series number, so reading the VIN can verify authenticity. Be aware that sometimes the VIN and data plates can be switched from one car to another during restoration. An owner may have a wrecked

1965 GTO convertible and an excellent 1965 Le Mans convertible body shell. Instead of rebuilding the wrecked 1965 GTO body, he may simply swap plates with the 1965 Le Mans. Depending on the quality of the handiwork, it

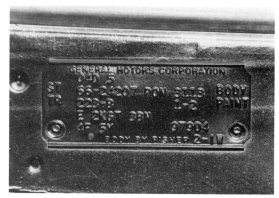

The data plate is located on the firewall of all 1964–1967 and 1974 GTO models. From 1968 through 1973, the plate was mounted on the LH side of the cowl, just beneath the hood hinge. Information on this plate includes paint and interior information, the assembly date, and model series information.

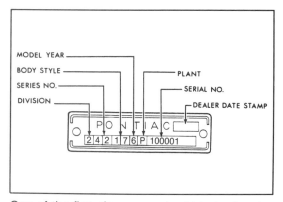

One of the first places you should look when inspecting a potential purchase is the VIN plate. From 1964 until 1967 it was located on the driver's side of the door pillar post. This VIN plate for a 1966 GTO indicates it was the first GTO (42 series) built at the Pontiac assembly plant.

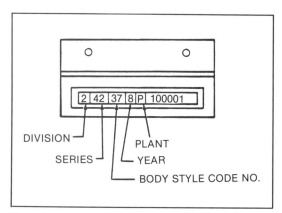

The VIN plate was moved to the top of the instrument panel in 1968 and located directly under the windshield where it's more easily seen and harder to remove or replace. This VIN identifies the first 1968 GTO coupe built at the Pontiac assembly plant.

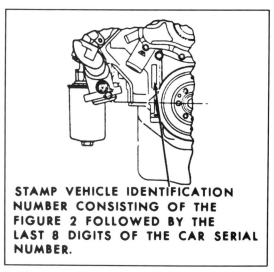

STAMP VEHICLE IDENTIFICATION NUMBER CONSISTING OF THE FIGURE 2 FOLLOWED BY THE LAST 8 DIGITS OF THE CAR SERIAL NUMBER.

Pontiac stamped engine coding on the RH front of the block. On 1964 models, the information consists of engine and transmission application and engine serial number. After 1965, only the engine code was stamped, along with engine serial number.

may be impossible to detect if the plates have been riveted to the body. If you have any doubts as you examine these items, walk away from the purchase, because the car might have been stolen somewhere down the line. Don't disregard this possibility; it may burn you when you go to sell the vehicle.

In 1972, the GTO again became an option on the Le Mans, and again you need to confront the problem of counterfeiting. Fortunately, the engine code was incorporated into the VIN, allowing the purchaser to compare the coded engine in the car with the engine code in the VIN. Any disparity here is grounds for scratching a car as a potential purchase.

In 1973 and 1974, the GTO was an option, first on the Le Mans and then the compact Ventura. Engine codes were again part of the VIN. Only two engines were offered in 1973, the code T 400ci 4bbl and the code Y 455ci 4bbl. In 1974, only the code B 350ci engine was offered. For a complete explanation of how to decipher data plate information on 1964–1974 GTOs, refer to the GTO Recognition Guide, available from Classic Motorbooks.

The GTO Judge, offered from 1969 to midyear 1971, has also been the subject of counterfeiting. Because there is no coding in the VIN or on the data plate to identify the Judge, and since it uses the same Ram Air engines as the GTO, all that is necessary to convert a GTO into a Judge is to add the appropriate stripes and decals, apply a Judge emblem to the glovebox door, add a rear spoiler, remove the trim rings from the Rally II wheels, and black out the grille.

Of course, the best way to determine a GTO's authenticity is to use the services of Pontiac Historical Services. While PHS is not a part of Pontiac Motor Division, it does have access to the billing invoices, and it is here you can verify if that 1964–1965 or 1972 GTO is really a GTO, or if the 1971 GTO Judge convertible (one of seventeen built) is real or fake. It also can help you spot engine or transmission swaps. A 1969 GTO with the base engine isn't worth nearly as much as a Ram Air IV version, but it takes only a few parts and two decals to make the conversion. The billing invoice will always tell the tale.

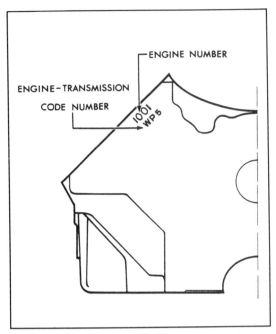

Beginning in 1968, the information was located on a machine pad next to the water pump. There the engine code was stamped along with the figure 2 and the last eight digits of the vehicle identification number.

This cylinder head is coded "48" (note numbers above center ports). It is used on the 1969 GTO Ram Air III and the 1969 Grand Prix 428. Note the date code just to the right and above the center ports. This is the casting date code for the head. It reads "L168," indicating it was cast on December 16, 1968. The date built code on the data plate of this GTO should indicate that the car was built approximately one week or more after the head was cast. If the head cast date is later than the car's date build code, then it is not the original head.

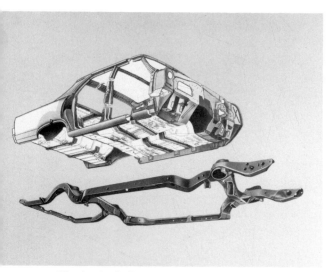

The body shell can have its share of rust problems. The floor- and trunkpans can rust out if there is leakage from the front and rear glass. Rust around the back window is also common, especially on 1968–1973 models. Another common area for rust is at the bottom of the quarter panels and the back of the rear wheelhouse opening.

What to Look For

The 1964–1973 GTOs were composite body/frame cars. In other words, the body was mounted on a separate frame, using rubber bushings to reduce shock transmission to the body. The front inner and outer fenders, radiator support, grilles and grille divider panel were then mounted to the body and/or frame.

The frame was a perimeter design, with two permanent crossmembers and a third bolted in to support the transmission. Torque boxes added additional stiffening. Convertibles were equipped with boxed frames (which could also be ordered optionally on coupes and hardtop models). The rear suspension was a four-link design with upper and lower control arms, coil springs, and tubular hydraulic shocks. Beginning in 1970, a rear antisway bar was installed. Up front, unequal-length control arms were used, along with coil springs, tubular hydraulic shocks, and an antisway bar. The 1974 GTO was based on the Ventura, which used unit-body

Most GTOs weren't pampered by their owners. As musclecars, they were used for high-performance driving, both on the street and the strip. Look for modifications to the front and rear suspension. In stock class racing it's popular to remove components to lighten the load, so inspect carefully for stripped parts.

construction like the Nova. It had a subframe attached to the front of the body.

GTOs that spent their lives in the North and were driven in the winter can have severe rust damage from road salt that is spread to melt snow and ice. Rust damage due to airborne salt can also be found on cars that lived in coastal areas. Those frame areas especially prone to rust are the rear crossmember (pay extra attention to the upper coil spring mounts) and the frame rails under the rockers.

Frame rot is difficult to repair. In severe cases, the frame should be replaced, which is costly, time consuming, and should be considered only if the GTO it's attached to is a significantly rare or desirable model. Keep in mind that frames are also coded and dated.

Coil spring sag is a common problem with all 1964–1973 GTOs. You can count on having to replace the springs. Fortunately, replacements are easy to find. The chances of the original gray, spiral-design Delco shock absorbers being intact are also slim, since the originals lasted only 25,000 miles, and most GTO owners didn't replace them with original equipment shocks.

The body shell has a variety of rust-prone areas. Around the lower rear window, water entered the body through the trim molding clip piercings. This area was especially bad in 1966–1967 because of the flat deck and the angled backlight. This water would pool and then find its way into the trunk. Plastic trunk mats were standard, and they would retain moisture between the mat and trunkpan. Eventually, oxidation would eat out the metal. The worst areas were in the cavities on each end of the trunkpan where the quarter panels roll in. Check the bottom of the quarters behind the wheel openings as well as inside the rear of the wheelhouse. Another problem area is just behind the left-hand side wheelhouse weld, where the body-to-frame bolt is located. Not only does the pan rust here, but severe rust can break the pan loose from the bolt.

Occasionally, the rear deck itself will be rotted (again most prevalent on 1966–1967). Decklids are also prone to rust on 1968–1972 models along the inside leading edge of the rear. Rust can also form around the taillamp assemblies. This was bad in 1967 and 1969.

Door skins can also be rusted through at the bottoms. A drain was located at the bottom of the doors, but if the drain hole was plugged by leaves or other debris, the water had nowhere to go. There is generally little rust around the door handles or hinges, and tops held up pretty well, but those models equipped with the optional vinyl roof could develop rust if the top was torn or nicked and water got between the vinyl and the metal.

One of the most common rust areas on GTOs is at the bottom of the front fenders behind the wheel openings. Leaves and pine needles and other debris accumulate there over a period of years, and since the area behind the fenders has no drainage and can't be cleaned out, the fender can rot out at this location.

Radiator core support panels at the frame mounts can be rusted, as can those areas around the headlamp buckets and front bumpers on 1964–1967 models. Occasionally, hoods will be rusted if the original underhood sound deadener is still in place and moisture has accumulated there. The hoods on 1968–1972 models have a tendency to bend at the hood hinge attachments. Floorpans can also rust, especially on manual transmission models. There can be considerable rust to the pans on the passenger side if the windshield

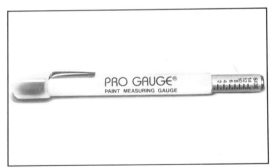

Both the Spot Rot autobody damage guide and the Pro Gauge paint measuring guide should be in every GTO buyer's toolbox. These two inexpensive gauges (the Spot Rot is $12.95, and the Pro Gauge is $35) can save you literally thousands of dollars by detecting plastic filler used to repair body damage and by determining if a car has been repainted. They are both available from Pro Motorcar Products, 22025 US 19N, Clearwater, FL 34625.

leaked. If a windshield leak was severe, gaping holes in the cowl under the bottom of the windshield on either side might also be present.

These are only the most common locations for rust, and the buyer of an original, nonrestored GTO needs to inspect each and every square inch of the car. Putting the car on a hoist and checking the undercarriage is also essential to locating any potential rust areas as well as frame damage due to collision.

But what if the car has been restored? Here the buyer must be extra careful. What kinds of repairs were made to these most common rust-prone areas? The ever-popular use of plastic filler should be checked by using a Spot Rot gauge. Using plastic filler to repair rustouts is unacceptable and should be read as an indication that other shortcuts may have been made during the bodywork phase of the restoration. Plastic filler is acceptable only as a skim when working out uneven surfaces on doors or quarter panels and not to replace holes or damaged metal.

Metal so badly damaged that it rusted out must be replaced. Fortunately for the GTO restorer, replacement body panels are available, as well as patch panels, trunkpans and some floorpans. Quality panel or patch replacement work is hard to detect if it is finished properly. In the trunk area, pan or quarter panel work is covered up by spatter paint on all models except the 1964. You won't be able to detect trunkpan replacement from underneath because of the fuel tank. Check those areas around the front and rear glass (look inside the rear window and the package shelf for water stains). Check the seams between doors, fenders, hood, and deck lid. Hanging the front end sheet metal on a GTO requires skill. Makes sure the intersection between the cowl panel, hood, and fenders is even. Inspect the wheel houses for repair. Undercoating, which was used on most GTOs, may hide repairs here. Get under the car and look at the floorpans for weld marks (again, fresh undercoating will hide this).

How well was the car painted? First check the paint code on the firewall or cowl data plate. Does it match? If not, remember an incorrect color will work against you when you sell the car. What kind of paint was used?

Lacquer, acrylic, or urethane? Lacquer paint jobs are getting scarce because of EPA standards and the new type of equipment needed to apply them. Most paint jobs are now urethane, which is acceptable by most judging standards as long as it looks like a factory application.

If the car was restored correctly, the original paint and primer was stripped to bare sheet metal and the car was primed and repainted. A good paint job will be about 4–5mils thick. You can check paint thickness with a Pro Gauge, a pocket-sized tool that accurately measures paint depth. Use the gauge and examine various areas around the car for paint thickness uniformity. If there's more than a 0.5ml difference, look closely at that area. If you find areas with a 1–1.5mils difference, it's possible the area was repainted on top of other paint. Paint that measures more than 6ml has most probably been applied over old paint. Cracking, peeling, and other problems may manifest themselves in a short period of time with paint this thick.

Also inspect the door jambs for repainting, and peel back the trunk weatherstripping and look closely around the jacking instruction decals under the deck lid. This can tell you if the car was taped and repainted. Look for overspray on the frame or in the engine compartment. The key here is to be smarter than the painter. Unless the car was stripped and disassembled and all the chrome and trim removed you will most certainly find evidence of repainting.

When inspecting the interior, look first at the carpet, especially around the footwells. Is it worn? Remove the door sill plates, and peel back the carpet and inspect the jute and the trunkpans. Is there evidence of water damage from a leaking windshield? Now crawl under the instrument panel, and using a flashlight, inspect the wiring. Is there a lot of splicing? It's possible that the car was originally equipped with standard gauges and a Rally Gauge was installed during the restoration. Bad wiring can start a fire that can gut a car in a matter of minutes.

Now look at the door panels, weatherstripping, and window felts. Check the installation of the console to make sure it's straight. From 1964 until 1969, Pontiac used Morrokide vinyl for seat coverings. It was extremely durable and wear resistant. In fact, it's not unusual for the stitching to give out before the material. Beginning in 1970, Pontiac switched to a knitted vinyl and then later even cheaper upholstery that tended to wear out quickly. Check under the seat upholstery. Are the seats recovered, and if so, how well do the upholstery patterns line up? The headliner should have no sags or stains, and the bows should line up properly. Also examine the package shelf, seat belts (they are coded), quarter trim panels, window cranks and door release handles, dashpad, and mirrors. The steering wheel should be straight when the wheels are true, and there should be little play in the wheel. Don't forget little things like the pedals (Chevy pedal pads slip right on but look a lot different) and the cowl kick panels.

Mechanically, you should examine the steering, brakes, suspension, and drivetrain. Drive the car and listen carefully to the engine. Feel the steering through the wheel. Is it loose, or is there a vibration transmitted through the wheel? That could indicate loose steering components. The brakes should stop the car straight with no noise or squealing. Pontiac engines are famous for loose timing chains. If the engine has more than 60,000 original miles and has never been rebuilt, you've got at least a timing chain, camshaft, and lifters in your future, even if you don't plan on doing a major engine rebuild.

While the car is on the hoist, look over the drivetrain. Look for leaks around the rear seal and damage to the oil pan. Check the transmission code for correctness. You can also determine the rear axle's correctness by reading the information on the axle tube. Check the fuel and brake lines, especially at the wheel cylinders, where leakage can be detected on the backing plate and the tire. Uneven tire wear indicates front end problems that an alignment may not cure.

If you are buying a car that you will be restoring, some of these faults are acceptable, since you will be tearing the car down and replacing or repairing much of the damage. Factor the amount of time, parts, and work needed to replace or repair, and then calculate this into the asking price of the car. If the total is higher than you feel the car will be worth or exceeds your planned budget, then look for another car.

If you find indications of trouble, poorly done work, or covered up damage, factor this into the price of the car. If the seller won't work with you on reducing the asking price, you're better off passing. A GTO in top condition, restored or not, is worthy of a fair market price. The amount of work you will have to put into the car is commensurate with the car's condition. Paying more for a concours-quality GTO can be worth every cent, since no further investment will be necessary to bringing the car up to top condition. A bargain-priced GTO is no bargain if you have to pour a wad of money and time into it to make it show quality. The saying, "You pays your money and you takes your chances," shouldn't apply when buying any car.

Rating Chart			
Star Code	Rating	Supply	Demand
★★★★★	Excellent	Limited	Highest
★★★★	Very Good	Below Average	High
★★★	Good	Average	Above Average
★★	Fair	Above Average	Average
★	Poor	High	Low

Chapter 2

1964–1965 GTO

★★★★★	1964–1965 Royal Bobcats
★★★★★	1964–1965 Tri-Power convertibles
★★★★	1964–1965 Tri-Power coupes
★★★★	1964–1965 Tri-Power hardtops
★★★★	1964–1965 4bbl convertibles
★★★	1964–1965 4bbl coupes
★★★	1964–1965 4bbl hardtops

When the Pontiac GTO appeared on the market on October 1, 1963, it introduced a new term to the automotive encyclopedia: musclecar. No one before had ever dropped a big-car engine into a midsized car and put together a package that appealed to young male drivers. The GTO was also affordable, and, thanks to

The 1964 GTO came in two closed body styles, hardtop and pillared coupe. This coupe is owned by Pontiac Motor Division, who performed the restoration in 1985.

The GTO lineup also included a convertible version. A vinyl boot covered the folded softtop. Red line 7.50x14 US Royal tires were a standard part of the GTO package.

an option list "as long as your arm and twice as hairy" (to quote Pontiac), the buyer could tailor his GTO to his individual taste.

Three body styles were offered: coupe, convertible, and hardtop. A buyer could order a coupe with the top-performance engine, close ratio four-speed gear box, 3.90:1 rear gears, and little else. The boulevard cruiser could buy a convertible and ladle on the goodies, including air conditioning, power windows, tilt wheel, and other luxury options. Even the bag boy at the local Safeway could afford a base engine GTO hardtop, and he'd have a prestigious ride through the high school parking lot.

Two engines were offered in the 1964 GTO. The base engine displaced 389ci and was rated at 325hp, thanks to a Carter AFB four-barrel carburetor and mild hydraulic camshaft. Pontiac engines were known for their train-pulling torque, and the base engine

Chromed exhaust splitters that exited behind the rear wheels were optional in both 1964 and 1965.

could easily spin the tread off the red line US Royal Tiger Paws, much to the delight of the drive-in crowd.

The top-of-the-line engine was also 389 cubes and shared the same heads, camshaft, and valvetrain with the base engine. Up top, however, was Pontiac's legendary Tri-Power—three two-barrel Rochesters topped by three tiny chrome air cleaners and tied to a vacuum-operated linkage. When the throttle was mashed to the floor, those three Rochesters would inhale so deeply it sounded like they would suck the hood clean into the engine. It was rated at 348hp. With the three

The Royal Bobcat

Although a lot of new car dealers were in the performance business back in the Sixties, few could compare to Royal Pontiac. Owned by Ace Wilson, Jr., Royal was a small Pontiac dealership just a few miles from Pontiac's headquarters in Royal Oak, Michigan. Thanks to the efforts of Jim Wangers, a member of Pontiac's advertising agency, Royal became the "backdoor" developer of what were advertised as the "Hot Chiefs". It was also the home of the Bobcat, a specially packaged 1961 Catalina that could outperform most performance cars. Royal also offered all the top Pontiac performance parts as well as a full inventory of aftermarket parts.

With the advent of the GTO in 1964, Royal shifted the Bobcat label to specially prepared GTOs. The Bobcat package was developed by mechanic Frank Reddicker, salesman Dick Jesse and Wangers. The Bobcat received special engine modifications that included a reworked distributor, larger carburetor jetting, thinner head gaskets, special fiber lock nuts to reduce lifter pump-up and Royal Bobcat decals that were placed on the C-pillars in 1964-1965, the front fenders in 1966-67 and on the doors (along with a special stripe) in 1968-1969.

Not only did Royal prepare all the GTOs that were placed in the hands of the automotive press, but many articles in those magazines on how to improve the GTO's horsepower were written with the assistance for Royal's team of mechanics, headed by Milt Schornack and Dave Warren. Because of these articles, Royal became the mecca of Pontiac Performance, and scores of young buyers would travel from all over the country to buy a Royal Bobcat from Dick Jesse (a successful drag racer himself). From 1964-1969, Royal produced a number of Bobcat-tuned GTOs.

Because of Royal's reputation, the performance modifications they made to the Bobcat GTOs and the small number produced, a genuine GTO Bobcat today is a highly desired collectable. When considering a Bobcat for purchase, there are three factors to consider. First, not all GTOs purchased from Royal were Bobcats; only those cars that were sent through the service department to have the special performance modifications added are considered Bobcats. Second, during its heyday, Royal sponsored the "Royal Racing Team" that could be joined for $3 and included a Royal decal and other items. GTO owners often place these Royal decals on their cars in hopes of making their friends think they, too, owned a Royal Bobcat. Problem was, without the engine modifications, it was just another GTO. Third, when considering a Bobcat for purchase, documentation is absolutely necessary, and that documentation must be an original bill of sale from Royal or other proof that the car not only was purchased from Royal Pontiac but also received the optional Bobcat performance option.

Royal Bobcats were specially modified GTOs sold by Royal Pontiac in Royal Oak, Michigan. Bobcats received this emblem, installed on the C-pillars of 1964–1965 GTOs.

separate chrome air cleaners and chrome valve covers, the GTO's engine looked as awesome as it performed.

Pontiac offered four transmissions for the GTO. The first was the standard three-speed box with floor-mounted Hurst shifter (the GTO was the first production car to be fitted with a Hurst shifter for all manual gearboxes).

Two four-speeds were optional, either a wide-ratio M20 or the close-ratio M21. The fourth, and least popular choice among the optional transmissions, was a two-speed Powerglide automatic.

Since GM had capped engine displacement in its midsized cars at 330ci, Pontiac had found a way of circumventing the rules by of-

The 1964 GTO's success contributed to the overall prosperity at Pontiac Motor Division. This Cameo Ivory GTO, which broke Pontiac's 1963 sales record of 590,072 units on June 1, 1964, was assembled at the Pontiac assembly plant. At far right is Elliot "Pete" Estes, Pontiac's general manager, who had the courage to sneak the GTO option through, although it technically broke GM's edict on engine displacement in its midsize products.

One of a Kind

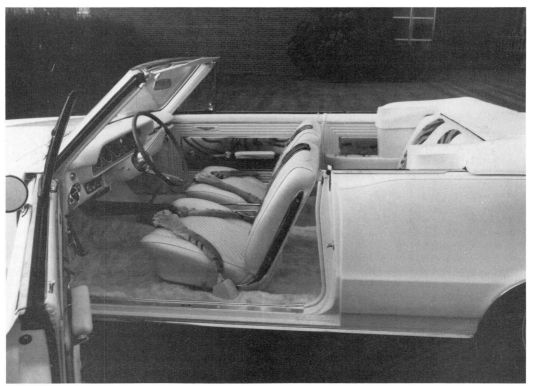

Few GTO show cars were built and displayed by Pontiac, and even less survive today. This is the Grand Marque V 1965 GTO show car. While this convertible looks stock on the outside (the wire wheel covers were a factory option), the interior more than makes up for it. This wild interior featured tiger-striped inserts in the door panels, quarter trim panels, and rear seat back.

Tiger paws cover the seatbelts. The GTO was known as the "GeeTO Tiger," a name that Pontiac never could get the public excited about.

This car still exists and belongs to a GTO collector in the Midwest. A GTO this unique is a rare find, and its value is far above any production car.

fering the GTO as an option package on the Le Mans. The GTO came standard with the 389 engine, heavy-duty suspension, and dual exhausts, along with special hood with twin dummy scoops, GTO nameplates on the LH grille, quarter panel and RH decklid, and a handsome triangular emblem mounted on the front fenders behind the wheel openings. Another GTO emblem was installed on the dash, along with an engine-turned aluminum applique on the instrument panel.

1964 GTO Production Figures

Body Style	Production	Engine	Trans.
Coupe	7,384	NA	NA
Hardtop	18,422	NA	NA
Convertible	6,644	NA	NA
Total	32,450		
1964	8,245	389-3x2	NA
1964	24,205	389-4bbl	NA
Total	32,450		

The 1964 GTO grilles were blacked out and the nameplate was in the left-hand grille.

The GTO nameplate appeared on the rear of the quarter panels.

1964 GTO Engine Codes

Engine ci	Carb. Type	Trans. Type	Std. Code	Calif. Code	Comp. Ratio	HP
389	3x3	3-Spd	76X	—	10.75:1	348
389	3x2	4-Spd	76W	—	10.75:1	348
389	3x2	4-Spd M20	76XW*	—	10.75:1	348
389	3x2	4-Spd M21	769	—	10.75:1	348
389	3x2	Auto	77J	—	10.75:1	348
389	4bbl	3-Spd	78X	—	10.75:1	325
389	4bbl	4-Spd M20	78W	—	10.75:1	325
389	4bbl	4-Spd M20	78XW*	—	10.75:1	325
389	4bbl	4-Spd M21	789	—	10.75:1	325
389	4bbl	Auto	79J	—	10.75:1	325

Total Production 389 3x2 Engine: 8,245
Total Production 389 4bbl Engine: 24,205
* To use leftover three-speed blocks the factory stamped a letter (W) after the (X) to mark them as four-speed blocks.

Twin dummy hood scoops were standard on the GTO hood. Made from cast metal, they are prone to pitting. Reproductions are available.

1964 GTO Exterior Colors and Codes

Color	Code
Starlight Black	A
Cameo Ivory	C
Silvermist Gray	D
Yorktown Blue	F
Skyline Blue	H
Pinehurst Green	J
Marimba Red	L
Sunfire Red	N
Aquamarine	P
Gulfstream Aqua	Q
Alamo Beige	R
Saddle Bronze	S
Singapore Gold	T
Grenadier Red	V
Nocturne Blue	W

Convertible Top Colors And Codes

Color	Code
Ivory	1
Black	2
Blue	4
Aqua	5
Beige	6
Saddle	7

Cordova Top Colors and Codes

Color	Code
Ivory	1
Black	2

Interior Colors and Codes

Color	Code
Black	214
Dark Blue	215
Light Saddle	216
Dark Aqua	217
Medium Red	218
Parchment	219

Note: All of the GTO's interior color components are of matching color with the exception of the parchment color option, which has white seats, door panels, headliner, sun visors, and windlace. The carpeting, kick panels, console base, package shelf, and dash pad are black.

1964 GTO Assembly Plant Codes

Code	Plant
BA	Baltimore
BF	Fremont
KC	Kansas City
PD	Pontiac

Several wheel cover options were offered in 1964. This is the three-piece Custom wheel cover with three-spoke spinner. A 7.50x14 red line tire was also standard.

Around back, a GTO nameplate was installed on the right-hand rear of the decklid. It is smaller then the grille or quarter panel nameplates.

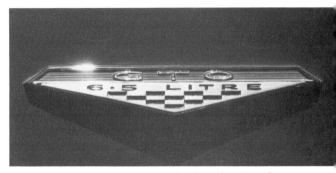

This GTO emblem appeared on the front fenders of 1964–1965 GTOs. Also cast from pot metal, it pitted quite easily. Originals are still available, but many of the castings are poor. If you purchase new ones in the box, inspect then immediately.

The GTO's interior was upscale, with full carpeting, thick-foam seats, and padded dash. This factory shot reveals a missing cover over the driver's seat belt retractor. Note the power seat switch on the driver's seat and GTO emblem over the glovebox door.

The four-pod instrument panel theme would be popular with GTOs for several years. This 1964 panel shows the engine-turned applique around the gauges. In the far right-hand pod is the optional tachometer.

The optional console was offered with box manual and automatic transmission-equipped GTOs. The console top featured a chrome rib motif that carried over to the storage compartment door. Hurst shifters were used in all manual transmission GTOs.

Buyers could load on the options if they so desired. This 1964 interior sports optional Custom Sport steering wheel, air conditioning, tilt column, and vacuum gauge on the console. Also installed is an AM/FM radio, not offered as factory equipment in 1964.

Somewhat overshadowed by Ford's phenomenal Mustang, GTO sales took off slowly. A controversial article in Car & Driver magazine, which stated the Pontiac GTO was every inch as much of a performer as its namesake, the Ferrari GTO, seemed to spark a surge in GTO sales, and when production closed out on Friday, July 31, 1964, 32,450 GTOs had been built.

The GTO had caught the competition flat-footed. No one was ready to field a GTO-class musclecar, and so Pontiac literally owned the market in 1965. It was ready with more improvements to the 1965 GTO, and buyers responded.

Since the 1964 models had scored high on style ballots conducted nationwide by GM's customer research staff and issued internally in January 1964, the Tempest series received only a facelift for 1965. The quad headlamps were now stacked vertically to emulate the big Pontiacs, and for the GTO, specific grilles were used. These deeply recessed grilles were blacked out and the left-hand grille carried a GTO nameplate. Around back, specific taillamp bezels were used, with six chromed ribs to trim the bezels. This six rib theme was carried over on the trim plate running across the rear where the name PONTIAC appeared in block letters.

GTO emblems again appeared on the quarter panels and decklid, with the GTO crest on the fenders. A new hood with a sin-

The GTO's trunk was spacious. Shown is the standard trunk mat and optional matching spare tire cover. Note that the trunk area is painted body color. After 1964, trunks would be finished with a spatter or fleck paint.

The standard 389ci four-barrel engine in 1964 came with chrome valve covers and air cleaner. It was rated at 325hp.

The optional engine was the Tri-Power, also displacing 389 cubes. Rated at 348hp, the Tri-Power got its name from the three Rochester two-barrel carburetor induction system. A vacuum-operated linkage tied the center and outer carbs together.

The 1965 GTO hardtop was the most popular model in the lineup, selling 55,722 units. Part of the GTO's appeal was its clean lines and tasteful lack of chrome trim. The 1965 is one of the most popular years among GTO fans.

gle simulated bubble scoop was also special for the GTO. Stamped steel Rally wheels were optional, as were chrome exhaust "splitters" that exited out the side behind the rear wheels.

Inside, the GTO shared the Le Mans interior, with full floor carpeting, luxurious Morrokide upholstery, cigar lighter, vinyl covered door panels, and dome light. The GTO received special touches, like GTO emblems on the door panels, a GTO nameplate on the passenger grab bar, and a wood applique on the instrument panel.

New options for 1965 included AM/FM radio, three-spoke Custom Sports steering wheel, and Rally Gauges, which placed a fuel gauge, 120mph speedometer, 8000rpm tachometer, water temperature, and oil pressure gauges in the four-pod instrument cluster. During the model year, the face of the tachometer was changed to show a 5200rpm red line, supposedly at the insistence of Pontiac's engine warranty department.

1965 GTO Production Figures

Body Style	Production	Engine	Trans.
Coupe	8,319	NA	NA
Hardtop	55,722	NA	NA
Convertible	11,311	NA	NA
Total	75,352		
1965	20,547	289-3x2	NA
1965	54,805	389-4bbl	NA
Total	75,352		
1965	56,378	NA	Manual
1965	18,974	NA	Auto
Total	75,352		

1965 GTO Engine Codes

Engine ci	Carb. Type	Trans. Type	Std. Code	Calif. Code	Comp. Ratio	HP
389	3x2	Manual	WS	—	10.75:1	360
389	3x2	Auto	YR	—	10.75:1	360
389	4bbl	Manual	WT	—	10.75:1	335
389	4bbl	Auto	YS	—	10.75:1	335

Total Production 389 3x2 Engine: 20,547
Total Production 389 4bbl Engine: 54,805
* Although never shown in production figures, over-the-counter and possibly dealer-installed Ram Air packages were sold for the 1965 GTO.

1965 GTO Transmission Codes

Transmission Description	Code
Three-Speed Manual Floor Shift X	
Three-Speed Manual Floor Shift H.D.	S
Four-Speed Manual Wide-ratio (M20)	W
Four-Speed Manual Close-ratio (M21) 4bbl	9
Four-Speed Manual Close-ratio (M21) 3x2bbl	8 or 9
Automatic (Powerglide)	J
Automatic (Powerglide) with Air Conditioning	T

1965 GTO Exterior Colors and Codes

Color	Code
Starlight Black	A
Blue Charcoal	B
Cameo Ivory	C
Fontaine Blue	D
Nightwatch Blue	E
Palmetto Green	H
Reef Turquoise	K
Teal Turquoise	L
Burgundy	N
Iris Mist	P
Montero Red	R
Capri Gold	T
Mission Beige	V
Bluemist Slate	W
Mayfair Maize	Y

Others

1 A SPEC=A standard GM paint color that was not offered by Pontiac.
2 A SPEC=A purely special paint / Tiger Gold Poly.
3 A SPEC=A Cadillac Firefrost color.
4 A SPEC=A car that was not painted at the factory but had been primed for painting at a later date.

Convertible Top Colors and Codes

Color	Code
White	1
Black	2
Blue	4
Turquoise	5
Beige	6

Cordova Top Colors and Codes

Color	Code
Black	2
Beige	6

1965 GTO Interior Colors and Codes

Color	Code
Black	213-30
Turquoise	214-36
Gold	215-34
Red	216-35
Blue	217-33
Parchment & Black	218-3E

1965 GTO Assembly Plant Codes

Code	Plant
A	Atlanta
B	Baltimore
G	Framingham
K	Kansas City
P	Pontiac
R	Arlington
Z	Fremont

The big news was under the hood. Pontiac upped the base engine power to 335hp. A new pancake-style chrome air cleaner was used on four-barrel engines. The Tri-Power's rating was now 360hp, thanks to a new camshaft, more efficient intake design, and redesigned intake ports for the heads. Also, stick-shift Tri-Powers were now equipped

The GTO also received specific taillamps that differed from the Le Mans in the number of ribs trimming the lens. The GTO had six, the Le Mans had ten.

with a mechanical accelerator linkage, while automatic models still used the vacuum setup.

Five transmissions were offered. Two three-speeds, one base and the other a heavy-duty option built by Ford; the M20 wide-ratio and M21 close ratio four-speeds; and the two-speed Powerglide automatic. Rear axle ratios now included a 4.33:1 for the serious drag racer. Underneath, there was little change to the suspension, steering, or brakes, although aluminum front drums were now optional to improve braking.

Pontiac had estimated sales in the 50,000 range for 1965. These projections were soon changed, even though GM had suffered a strike in the early part of the model year that ended in November. By the end of the model year, 75,352 1965 GTOs were roaming the streets. No other car maker (with the exception of the Mustang) had come even close to selling as many performance cars as the GTO.

Best Buys

While most of the perils of buying a thirty-year-old car were covered in chapter 1, some further details apply to the 1964–1965 GTOs.

First, be sure to inspect the car's codes and dates. Most GTO owners are aware of

The 1965 GTO received specific grilles, which were recessed and blacked out. The GTO nameplate again appears in the left-hand grille. Vertically stacked headlamps were new in 1965.

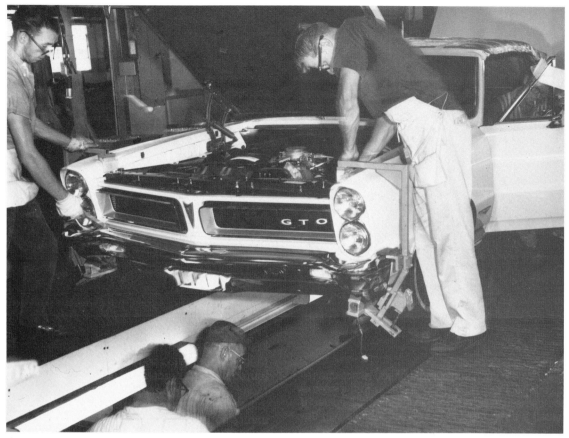

On the final assembly line at the Pontiac home plant, this 1965 GTO convertible is being fitted with front fenders. Note the overspray on the upper corner of the firewall.

the billing invoices available through Pontiac Historical Services and may have taken the time to document their cars. If they have the documentation in their hands when you examine the car, you can be assured of the car's authenticity.

Second, pay special attention to the car's condition. A number of value guides (such as the CPI value book) and listings in Hemmings Motor News allow you to gauge current values based on options and condition. These guides are based on asking prices and auction results and provide baseline information. The listings in Hemmings are asking prices and do not reflect the final negotiated selling price.

The standard hub cab for 1965. Depending on the exterior color of the car, wheels were either painted black or body color. Red line US Royal 7.75x14 bias ply tires were standard.

When it comes to investment or even for the sheer fun of driving, the Tri-Power engine option should be the GTO buyer's first choice. The Tri-Power-equipped convertibles are the rarest, and some were loaded from the factory with four-speed gearbox and air conditioning. These are the favorites of GTO collectors. Considering their low production and excellent performance, they are gold-plated investments that will always remain strong.

A few of the famous Royal Bobcats are still around, but again, they must be documented with paperwork from Royal to be authentic. Since Royal was located outside of Detroit, most of these cars turn up in central and eastern Michigan. It's also important to define a Royal Bobcat. Just because a GTO was purchased from Royal, does not make it a Royal Bobcat. Bobcats received special modifications from Royal mechanics and were con-

A UAW strike at the beginning of the model year slowed 1965 production. By late November production was back up to full speed. The entire auto industry enjoyed a record-breaking 1965 model year. GTO sales broke the 75,000 unit mark, exceeding projections by 25,000 units. Cars shipped from the home plant in Pontiac traveled by rail to Florida, Massachusetts, New York, Georgia, Missouri, and Montana.

For 1965, the GTO interior was revised slightly. Upholstery patterns were changed, and featured a large Pontiac crest in the seat back. A wood applique faced the instrument panel, and a new Rally Gauge Cluster option placed instruments for fuel, temperature, oil pressure, tachometer and speedometer in the four gauge pods. Also shown is the three-spoke Custom Sport steering wheel. This four-speed GTO was ordered without console.

sidered a dealer option. Also, Bobcats came equipped with special decals on the C-pillars (in 1964 and 1965) that were not installed on regular GTOs sold by Royal.

Tri-Power coupes and hardtops are also desirable. These cars can be equipped with a variety of options, or they can be stripped, devoid of even power steering and power brakes. Here, condition plays a big part in determining price. A loaded Tri-Power coupe may not be worth as much as a stripped hardtop if the hardtop's condition is better. Also, the way the car is equipped may influence the buyer. A buyer may want a stripped Tri-Power four-speed GTO because it's like the one he or she had in high school.

Four-barrel models are far more common than Tri-Powers. Convertibles are again the

The door panel was trimmed in Morrokide vinyl and featured the GTO emblem. Power windows and remote control outside driver's side mirror were optional.

The standard engine for 1965 was a four-barrel 389ci powerplant rated at 335hp. The low-profile air cleaner was chromed with louvers around the diameter, similar in style to that used on the Corvette. The valve covers were also chromed. The power brake booster on this particular GTO is incorrectly finished.

best choice for investment. Coupes are rarer than hardtops, and more four-speed versions are around. The two-speed Powerglide was not as popular with GTO buyers in 1964 and 1965.

Remember that most GTOs went through a number of owners over the years, and few escaped modifications of one sort or another. No 1964–1965 GTOs were equipped with the 12-bolt rear differential, although a limited slip rear (Safe-T-Track) was offered. Also, only a front and rear package shelf speaker was offered. No speakers were located in the doors. Only one style of upholstery was offered in the GTO: the top-of-the-line Le Mans vinyl interior. There were no standard and deluxe interiors.

For those four-barrel GTOs sold in California, a positive crankcase ventilator was required. This required the use of a standard four-barrel air cleaner was snorkel. For GTOs, the air cleaner top was chromed. California Tri-Power engines used a small tube at the air cleaner base, which tied to a T fitting and then into the valve cover.

In August of 1965, Pontiac released an over the counter package dubbed cold air induction. The package included another hood scoop ornament that was opened and painted by the customer, instructions on how to cut away part of the underhood bracing, and a pan with foam seal that fitted on top of the carburetors. When the hood was closed, the seal fitted against the hood underside and sealed out hot engine compartment air, allowing only cold air from the open scoop to feed the carburetors. Known as Ram Air, this accessory is extremely rare and desirable. Reproductions of the pans have so far been made of fiberglass. The original pans were metal.

Chapter 3

1966–1967 GTO

The GTO's incredible popularity in its first two years caused Pontiac product planners to rethink the GTO's position in the division's model lineup. Because GM waived its corporate policy of capping engine displacement of midsized models at 330ci, Pontiac could now shuck the option status of the GTO and make it an independent series.

Still based on the Tempest series, the GTO continued to share much of the Le Mans' interior appointments and accessory option list. The exterior of the GTO was markedly different from the Le Mans. Twin recessed egg-crate grilles constructed of plastic (only the Grand Prix and the GTO used them in 1966) were split by a header panel. The blacked-out grilles featured a white-paint-filled nameplate in the LH grille and

★★★★★	1966 Royal Bobcats
★★★★★	1966 Tri-Power Ram Air (XS code)
★★★★★	1966 Tri-Power convertibles
★★★★	1966 Tri-Power coupes
★★★★	1966 Tri-Power hardtops
★★★★	1966 4bbl convertibles
★★★	1966 4bbl coupes
★★★	1966 4bbl hardtops
★★★★★	1967 Royal Bobcats
★★★★★	1967 Ram Air convertibles
★★★★★	1967 HO convertibles
★★★★	1967 Ram Air coupes
★★★★★	1967 Ram Air hardtops
★★★★	1967 HO coupes
★★★★★	1967 HO hardtops
★★★★★	1967 Base engine convertibles
★★★	1967 Base engine coupes
★★★	1967 Base engine hardtops
★★★	1967 2bbl convertibles
★★	1967 2bbl coupes
★★	1967 2bbl hardtops

1966 GTO Production Figures

Body Style	Production	Engine	Trans
Coupe	10,363	NA	NA
Hardtop	73,785	NA	NA
Convertible	12,798	NA	NA
Total	96,946		
1966	19,045	389-3x2	NA
1966	77,901	389-4bbl	NA
Total	96,946		
1966	61,279	NA	Manual
1966	35,667	NA	Auto
Total	96,946		

vertically stacked quad headlamps. The bumper was interchangeable with the Le Mans. The bubble scoop hood was carried over from 1965, along with the GTO emblems on the front fenders and quarter panels.

At the rear, a flat taillamp panel was adorned with the name PONTIAC in individual block letters, flanked by louvered taillamps. Bright work trimmed the wheel openings, windows, decklid, and taillamp louvers. The rear window was recessed, and the C pillars swept back, providing a semifastback appearance at profile. A Cordova grain vinyl top was optional on coupes and hardtops.

Inside, the seats were redesigned to provide more lateral support, with hard shell seat backs and headrests optional. Nylon twist carpeting stretched across the doors and up the lower sections of the doors. A small GTO emblem was affixed to the upper center of the door panel. The optional console was carried over from 1965, as was the optional Custom Sports steering wheel and tilt column.

The instrument panel was restyled, retaining the four-pod theme but with redesigned instrument faces and a genuine wood veneer applique. An instrument panel crash pad was standard. The Rally Gauge cluster was again offered as an option, as was AM/FM radio, four-way hazard flasher, power antenna, and rear-seat speaker with reverberation. A passenger grab bar was standard.

Mechanically, the GTO was little changed from 1965. The chassis, brakes, and suspension were carried over. Metallic brake linings and aluminum front drums were optional. Power trains were also unchanged. The base four-barrel engine was again rated at 335hp. The Tri-Power was pegged at 360hp.

This preproduction styling car captures the theme of the 1966 GTO. The look was broader, rounder, and smoother than 1965. The vertically set headlamps and split grille theme were distinctly Pontiac.

The deeply recessed grilles were constructed of plastic and were offered only on the GTO and Grand Prix.

1966 GTO Engine Codes

Engine Description	Std. Code	Calif. Code	Comp. Ratio	HP
4bbl Manual	WT	WW	10.75:1	335
4bbl Auto	YS	XE	10.75:1	335
3x2bbl Manual	WS	WV	10.75:1	360
3x2bbl Auto	YR	—	10.75:1	360
3x2bbl Manual RA*	XS	—	10.75:1	360

* Although never shown in production figures, there were approximately twenty-five to thirty-five factory-built 1966 Ram Air GTOs (XS Package). It is estimated that 300 dealer Ram Air packages were sold for 1966 GTOs.

The 1966 GTO convertible. Sales reached 12,798 units, making it the second most popular body style, surpassing the pillared coupe by over 2,000 units.

Two closed versions were offered, the pillared coupe and the hardtop (shown). The flanks were rounded and devoid of chrome trim with the exception of bright trim along the rockers and around the wheel openings. Thin louvers exposed the tail-lamps. Note the recessed back light and the semi-fastback appearance of the C-pillars.

1966 GTO Transmission Codes

Five different transmissions were available for a 1966 GTO, the standard being a three-speed manual located on the steering column. A three-speed manual with a Hurst floor-mounted shifter was also available. (This transmission was built by Ford and is identified by Ford's toploader design.) There were two choices of four-speed manual transmissions for 1966: a wide-ratio M20 four-speed was available for rear-end gear ratios up to 3.90. The other option was a close-ratio M21 four-speed available for cars equipped with 3.90 or 4.33 rear-end gear ratios. The only automatic transmission available for 1966 was the two-speed Powerglide, with the gear selector located on the steering column for standard versions and an optional floor-mounted shifter with console.

Transmission	Code
Column Shift Three-Speed Manual	5
Three-Speed Manual Floor Shift	S
Automatic (Powerglide)	J
Four-Speed Manual Wide-ratio (M20)	W
Four-Speed Manual Close-ratio (M21)	8

1966 GTO Exterior Colors and Codes

Color	Code
Starlight Black	A
Blue Charcoal	B
Cameo Ivory	C
Fontaine Blue	D
Nightwatch Blue	E
Palmetto Green	H
Reef Turquoise	K
Marina Turquoise	L
Burgundy	N
Barrier Blue	P
Montero Red	R
Martinique Bronze	T
Mission Beige	V
Platinum	W
Candelite Cream	Y

Convertible Top Colors and Codes

Color	Code
White	1
Black	2
Blue	4
Turquoise	5
Beige	6

The Rally wheel was available at extra cost. This stamped steel wheel was fitted with a bright trim ring and center cap with blacked-out dish. US Royal 7.75x14 red line tires were standard.

The spare tire was stored in the right-hand side of the trunk and retained by a bolt and wing nut. The two-piece trunk mat was made of plastic and was notorious for retaining moisture and promoting trunk-pan rust.

The GTO interior featured new Strato bucket seats covered with Morrokide vinyl and hard shell backs. The console was a carryover from 1965 and was again optional. There was only one level of interior trim for the GTO.

Cordova Top Colors and Codes

Color	Code
Ivory	1
Black	2
Beige	6

1966 GTO Interior Colors and Codes

Color	Code
Blue	219
Turquoise	220
Fawn	221
Red	222
Black	223
Parchment	224

The optional Rally Gauge cluster for 1966 placed the fuel gauge and battery telltale lamp in the far left pod, the 120mph speedometer and odometer in the center left, the 8000rpm tachometer in the center right, and the water temperature and oil pressure gauges in the far right. The Rally clock was not offered with the gauge package in 1966.

1966 GTO Assembly Plant Codes

Code	Plant
B	Baltimore
G	Framingham
K	Kansas City
P	Pontiac
Z	Fremont

Past the midpoint of the model year, Pontiac quietly offered a factory version of the Ram Air. This option, often known as the XS package (named after the engine designation), came with another scoop ornament that was to be opened to allow cold air to enter the hood, a Ram Air tub that sealed to the underhood, a hotter cam, and other engine hard-

The instrument panel was redesigned for 1966, with a larger fascia housing all the controls and switches. The optional Custom Sport steering wheel shown here was unchanged from 1965.

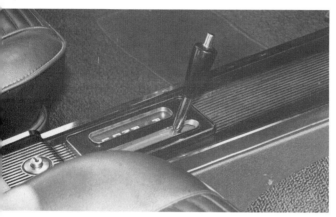

When a buyer ordered the center console with automatic transmission, Pontiac installed this shifter. It differs from the 1964–1965 shifter in that it uses a black plastic knob and chrome button to activate reverse and park detents.

ware. Less than thirty of these cars were produced. The package was similar to the 1965 cold air package offered over the counter, except this package was packed in the trunk and the 1965 package offered no camshaft.

The GTO continued to dominate the market in 1966. Pontiac had discovered how to tie in the GTO's name and image to other products—a brilliant marketing move that put the GTO name in stores, magazine ads, and other media. GTO cologne, shoes, jewelry, records, and other paraphernalia soon flooded the market, and the car's recognition grew far beyond the scope of just performance enthusiasts.

At the close of production on August 3, 1966, 96,946 GTOs had been built. That represented over 10 percent of total Pontiac sales in 1966. It would also be the high water mark for

The base engine for 1966 was the 335hp 389, topped by a Carter AFB four-barrel and using the same pancake-style air cleaner found on the 1965 base engine. The Tri-Power was virtually the same as in 1965, except that the center carburetor was enlarged to equal the outers. Air conditioning was available with both the four-barrel and Tri-Power engines.

the GTO; no other year would ever be as successful.

Production of 1967 GTOs began at the end of August 1966. For 1967, the only external changes were cosmetic. Up front, the plastic grilles were replaced with a mesh chrome design. The bright rocker panel was raised to cover the lower section of the door, and the GTO emblem was lowered and placed within the rocker panel. Around back, the rear was restyled with a new bumper. The decklid now ran flat across the rear, and the taillamps were changed to narrow quad lamps on each side. GTO nameplates still appeared in the LH grille, the quarter panels, and the RH rear of the deck lid.

The interior was also only slightly revamped. The door panels and seat upholstery were redesigned, as was the optional console (now covered with an imitation wood veneer that matched the instrument panel). Instrumentation was only slightly different from

The XS Ram Air option was a midyear package named after the engine code. All of the over-the-counter components of the cold air package were included in the trunk, however a stronger camshaft and stiffer valve springs and dampers were installed at the factory. Less than fifty of the XS engines were installed in 1966 GTOs.

A code YS GTO four-barrel engine awaits its turn to be installed at the Pontiac factory. The engines were assembled and dressed at the engine plant prior to shipment to the final assembly point.

Upstairs at the Pontiac assembly plant, painted GTO bodies stand in line among Le Mans and Tempests waiting for the body drop that will marry the completed chassis to the finished body shell.

1966, with a split turn signal indicator the major change. The optional Rally Gauge Cluster was still available, as was a hood-mounted tachometer.

Other new options included an 8-track player (mounted below the dash) and cruise control. The steering wheel was restyled, and the three-spoke Custom Sport steering wheel was almost identical to the 1965–1966 version. Federally regulated safety equipment was starting to appear in 1967; the steering column was wider in diameter thanks to its energy absorbing feature, and the four-way flasher was now standard and incorporated into the column.

1967 GTO Production Figures

Body Style	Production	Engine	Trans
Coupe	7,029	NA	NA
Hardtop	65,176	NA	NA
Convertible	9,517	NA	NA
Total	81,722		
1967	751	400 RA	NA
1967	2,967	400 2bbl	NA
1967	13,827	400 HO	NA
1967	39,128	NA	Manual
1967	42,594	NA	Auto
Total	81,722		

1967 GTO Engine Codes

Engine Description	Std. Code	Calif. Code	Comp. Ratio	HP
400 4bbl 3Spd Manual	WT	WW	10.75:1	335
400 HO 3Spd Manual	WS	WV	10.75:1	360
400 4bbl 4Spd	WT	WV	10.75:1	335
400 HO 4Spd	WS	WV	10.75:1	360
400 Ram Air Manual	XS	YR	10.75:1	360
400 4bbl Automatic	YS	—	10.75:1	335
400 2bbl Automatic	XM	XL	8.60:1	255
400 HO Automatic	YZ	—	10.75:1	360
400 Ram Air Automatic	XP	—	10.75:1	360

1967 GTO Transmission Codes

Five different transmissions were available for a 1967 GTO, the standard being a three-speed manual with a Hurst floor-mounted shifter. There were two choices of four-speed manual transmissions for 1967, a wide-ratio M20 four-speed was available for rear-end gear ratios up to 3.90:1. The other option was a close-ratio M21 four-speed available for cars equipped with 3.90:1 or 4.33:1 rear-end gear ratios. 1967 was the first year for the three-speed Hydra-Matic transmission. Available only on the GTO, the Hydra-Matic was used for all applications in 1967 (the 2bbl GTO motor used a differently coded Hydra-Matic).

Transmission	Code
Three-Speed Manual Floor Shift	S
Automatic (Hydra-Matic)	J
Four-Speed Manaul Wide-ratio (M20)	W
Four-Speed Manual Close-ratio (M21)	8
Automatic (Hydra-Matic 2bbl Engine Only)	X

1967 GTO Exterior Colors and Codes

Color	Code
Starlight Black	A
Cameo Ivory	C
Montreux Blue	D
Fathom Blue	E
Tyrol Blue	F
Signet Gold	G
Linden Green	H
Gulf Turquoise	K
Mariner Turquoise	L
Plum Mist	M
Burgundy	N
Silverglaze	P
Regimental Red	R
Champagne	S
Montego Cream	T

Convertible Top Colors and Codes

Color	Code
White	1
Black	2
Blue	4
Turquoise	5
Cream	7

Cordova Top Colors and Codes

Color	Code
Ivory	1
Black	2
Cream	7

There were significant changes to the GTO mechanically in 1967. The frame and suspension were basically unaltered, but a dual braking system was standard and front disc brakes were now offered optionally. Two

Final assembly at the Pontiac home plant. The front fenders have been attached to the radiator support and the body shell. As the car moved down the line, trim, engine compartment components, interiors, exhaust system, and bumpers were installed.

sport wheels were offered: the Rally I (unchanged from 1966) and the new five-spoke Rally II.

1967 GTO Interior Colors and Codes

Color	Code
Blue	219
Turquoise	220
Gold	221
Black	223
Parchment	224
Red	225
Black	235*
Parchment	236*

* The bench seat option was added to the regular line-up of interiors in 1967 with its own firewall ID number making it easier to

A Royal Bobcat launches off the line at Motor City Dragway. Royal Bobcats were specially prepared GTOs sold by Royal Pontiac that received engine modifications, adding to the sticker price of the car. Those GTOs fitted with Bobcat modifications were trimmed with a special decal located on the front fenders ahead of the wheel opening. The Hurst wheels were also available at extra cost from Royal.

identify the bench seat interior. The 1966 models require a factory invoice to identify.

1967 GTO Assembly Plant Codes

Code	Plant
B	Baltimore
G	Framingham
K	Kansas City
P	Pontiac
Z	Fremont

1967 GTO Ram Air Production

Manual	Automatic	Total
595	156	751

56 Ram Air convertibles were built.

The powertrain received major changes in 1967. The venerable 389 was drilled out to displace 400ci, and new heads with larger valves and redesigned combustion chamber were standard. For the first time, a low-compression, two-barrel carbureted engine rated at 255hp was offered for those who wanted to be seen driving a GTO but wanted fuel economy and little performance. The standard engine was rated at 335hp using the Rochester 4bbl Quadra-Jet carburetor. Next step up was the HO, rated at 360hp, thanks to a hotter cam, open air filter, and free-flowing exhaust manifolds.

Top dog was the 360hp Ram Air with Rochester Quadra-Jet, now offered from the factory with an extra hood scoop ornament that was opened by the dealer and an open air element air cleaner and tub that sat on the carburetor, sealing out hot underhood air. It was up to the customer or the dealer to install and paint the scoop ornament. The Ram Air also

One of the rarest options for the GTO convertible was this tonneau cover, which snapped into place. This shot was taken in the Pontiac Engineering Garage and shows an interesting experiment taking place. The car next to the convertible is a 1965 Le Mans equipped with the overhead cam six-cylinder engine (which was not offered until 1966) being fitted with 1966 fenders.

Looks like a GTO interior, doesn't it? This car is equipped with Custom Sport wheel, Rally Gauge cluster, and four-speed transmission, so it must be a GTO, right? It's not. These options were also offered on the Tempest and the Le Mans. Two clues indicate this is not a GTO. The door panels are from a Tempest and there is no wood applique over the instrument fascia. Also, the Tempest and Le Mans used a pebble-grain finish for the instrument panel cluster. Making a counterfeit GTO out of a 1966 Tempest or Le Mans is difficult, but it can be done since many of the same options were offered among the three series.

used the HO's exhaust manifolds and came with high lift cam and special valve springs. Toward the later part of the production year (on Ram Air GTOs with serial numbers 646616 and higher), the standard cast number 670 heads used on all 4bbl GTOs were replaced on the Ram Air engines with cast number 97 heads. These heads featured different valves and used special valve springs and taller valve spring stack heights.

Transmission choices started with the base three-speed with floor-mounted Hurst shifter. The wide-ratio M20 or close-ratio M21 four-speed transmissions were optional. The two-speed Powerglide was retired in favor of the bulletproof three-speed Turbo Hydramatic, which, when ordered with console, was shifted by the Hurst "His and Hers" shifter. The Hurst unit allowed the driver to shift through the gears him- or herself or leave it in drive. Rear ratios ran from a miserly 2.56:1 (on two-barrel versions) to stump-pulling 4.33:1 cogs.

Although the GTO was facing stiff competition in 1967, sales continued to be strong, with 81,722 satisfied customers. The competition, such as the SS396 Chevelle, Plymouth GTX, Dodge Super Bee, Oldsmobile 4-4-2, and Buick Gran Sport, still weren't chalking up the sales numbers enjoyed by the GTO, but some of them could beat the GTO on the street. Pontiac was still the undisputed leader of the musclecar market, and that leadership would continue for several more years.

The option that wasn't. Pontiac had planned to offer a 14in version of its popular eight-lug wheel for the Tempest/Le Mans/GTO. The option even appeared in ads and showroom brochures, but was canceled at the last minute. None of the Kelsey-Hayes wheels were ever installed on Pontiac's midsize cars.

Since the GTO became a separate series in 1966, the data plate on the firewall identifies this 1966 model as 24217 (a GTO hardtop). Other pertinent data includes build date (10A=the first week of October), interior color (223=black), paint (W2 - W=Platinum; 2= black top), and assembly location (BAL=Baltimore assembly plant).

The 1967 GTO carried over much of the previous year's styling, although subtle changes were made to the front, rear, and flanks. The grilles were now trimmed with a chromed wire mesh, and the rocker panel was raised up to cover the lower part of the door. Note the five-spoke Rally II wheels, a new option for 1967.

Both a coupe and hardtop version were offered in 1967. Options shown on this hardtop include Cordova vinyl top, power antenna, remote control outside rearview mirror, and wire wheel covers.

A hood-mounted tachometer was now available for 1967 GTOs. At the beginning of the model year it was a dealer-installed option, but later it was available as a regular production option. The tachometer was lit at night when the instrument panel lights were activated. Early units were prone to lens fogging due to inadequate moisture drainage and ventilation. That problem was solved in later years.

The GTO's rear taillamps were revised to feature twin lamps stacked two high. This design was prone to rust out around the lamps and the sheet metal. Note the GTO nameplate on the decklid.

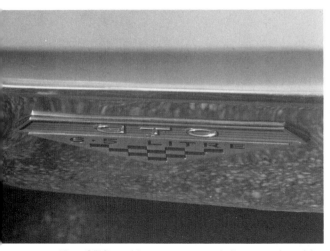

The GTO emblem was moved downward and incorporated into the rocker panel trim. Its styling is unchanged from 1964–1966.

The grille was now a two-piece assembly, with a chromed wire mesh trimming the grille opening. The simulated fog lamps were actually parking lamps.

The GTO cockpit was little changed from 1966. The steering column was thicker due to its energy-collapsing feature and the four-way flasher was incorporated into the column. The standard three-spoke steering wheel had horn buttons in the left and right spokes. The optional console was now covered with imitation wood trim to match the instrument panel.

The passenger grab bar with GTO nameplate was retained from 1966. Note the air conditioning vents in and under the dash and the optional three-spoke Custom Sports steering wheel.

While the Hurst Dual Gate shifter had been around for several years, Pontiac was the first to use it in a production car. When a buyer ordered the center console with automatic transmission, Pontiac included the Dual Gate. The Dual Gate (commonly referred to as the "His and Hers" shifter), allowed the driver to shift through first, second, and third gears or to leave the selector in drive and let the transmission shift itself.

What to Look Out For

Since the GTO was given series status, the VIN will clearly state whether the car you are inspecting is truly a GTO. If the first three characters of the VIN do not read 242, it's not a GTO but a Le Mans or Tempest in GTO clothing.

Because of the unique rear window design of the 1966–1967 GTO, water had a tendency to pool around the lower rear window frame. It would eventually rust out the holes retaining the window molding clips and drip down into the trunk. The sheet metal under

The Strato bucket seats and the door panels received new upholstery in 1967. The '67 also had seatback locks, a new safety feature. To pull the seatback forward, the button had to be depressed.

A smaller version of the GTO emblem was located on the upper center of the front door trim panels.

For the first time, a low-compression two-barrel engine was offered in the GTO. It was not widely received, selling only 2,967 copies at a time when engines with high compression and horsepower were king.

the deck and around the rear window will most likely be rotted or will have been repaired. You should take a flashlight, lie on your back in the trunk, and look closely at the underside of the deck in front, around the

The 1967 GTO engine line-up included two performance engine options. The HO option (left) included free-flowing exhaust manifolds, open air cleaner, high-lift camshaft, and stiffer valve springs. The Ram Air option (right and foreground) also used the same exhaust manifolds, different camshaft, stiffer valve springs and dampers, foam air cleaner, and a pan that fit over the carburetor base. The pan was fitted with a thick foam gasket, which sealed out hot underhood air when the hood was closed. The scoop ornament was open to allow cold outside air to tamp into the Rochester Quadra-Jet four-barrel carburetor.

The standard engine displaced 400ci and was rated at 335hp. New heads, an enlarged cylinder bore, and Rochester Quadra-Jet carburetor made up the biggest changes from 1966.

The HO (for High Output) was rated at 360hp. Notice the dual reservoir master brake cylinder, new for 1967. It was standard with or without power brakes. Front disc brakes were also offered optionally in 1967.

The Ram Air engine was somewhat underrated at 360hp. Because only one rear axle ratio was offered—4.33:1—with mandatory limited slip rear, air conditioning was not available with Ram Air.

rear window, and around the hood hinge attaching points for rust.

You should also carefully inspect the trunk. Check the cavity on either side of the trunkpan where the quarter panel rolls under. Water would collect there and rust out the bottoms of the quarters and the rear of the wheelhouse. Also, next to the wheelhouse in the trunk is a body-to-frame bushing bolt. Check the metal around the bolt for rot.

The trunkpan itself is prone to rust because the floor mat retained moisture. The factory used spatter (also known as "fleck") paint for the trunk, so repairs could have been made and covered with a fresh coat. Spend quite a bit of time in the trunk looking for rust

Side by side are the top-performance induction systems of the 1966 and 1967 GTOs. Traditionalists grieved when the legendary Tri-Power (left) was discontinued at the end of the 1966 production run. But when the Ram Air four-barrel Rochester Quadra-Jet was introduced in 1967, it didn't take performance fans long to appreciate the potential of the new system. One important point to note: Never

at any time did the Pontiac home plant or any of the satellite assembly plants install a Tri-Power induction system on a 1967 GTO and ship to a dealer for sale. No multiple carburetion setups were offered by Pontiac for the 1967 GTO. A dealer could install the Tri-Power at the customer's request, but all 1967 GTOs came from the factory with Rochester Quadra-Jets.

or rust repairs. Fortunately, replacement sheet metal is available for most of the areas around the trunk that were prone to rust in 1966–1967 GTOs.

Best Buys

When it comes to best buys, GTO enthusiasts are split between the Tri-Power and the Ram Air. It really comes down to personal preference, because both hold about the same value. While production breakdowns for 1966 remain cloudy, it is known that only 751 Ram Air GTOs were built in 1967 (56 were convertibles), making the Ram Air ragtop one of the most desirable of all 1967 GTOs.

For 1966, any Tri-Power convertible is most desirable, followed by the XS Ram Air option and Tri-Power coupes and hardtops. Proving that a 1966 was equipped with the XS engine option can be done only with a copy of the billing invoice. The 1967 Ram Air and HO coupes and hardtops are second only to the

The fenders are fitted to a 1967 GTO at the Pontiac home plant. The fenders were attached to the body shell cowl and the radiator support. Notice the firewall on this GTO. Part of the wall on the driver's side is painted body color (and covering the data plate), while the right hand side of the firewall is painted black.

A whole lot of GTOs and Pontiacs waiting to be shipped from the Pontiac assembly plant to dealers throughout the country. Big Pontiacs as well as midsize models were assembled on the same assembly line at Pontiac. Notice the protective plastic covering used on convertible tops.

By the end of the 1967 model year, the GTO had sold 81,722 units. Its combination of good looks and great performance had dominated the first four years of the musclecar era. Soon the competition would begin fielding musclecars that were faster and sometimes cheaper than the GTO. But in the end it was the twin specters of disapproval from safety groups and pressure from the insurance industry that put an end to the GTO and the musclecars it spawned.

convertibles with the top two engines. After that, the standard engine GTOs are popular. The 2bbl versions are oddities (2,967 built) and are not considered collectible.

Because Pontiac offered a wide array of options, buyers often opted to add accessories. One of the most unusual options offered in 1966–1967 was the red fender liners. These heavy plastic liners were shaped to fit inside the wheelhouses and kept dirt and road salt away from the body. Only 1,334 GTOs were ordered with the code 522 red fender liners in 1967. Keep in mind that rear axle ratios over 3.23:1 were not offered by the factory with air conditioning.

Chapter 4

1968–1969 GTO

★★★★★	1968 Royal Bobcats
★★★★★	1968 Ram Air convertibles
★★★★★	1968 Ram Air II hardtops
★★★★	1968 Ram Air hardtops
★★★★	1968 HO convertible
★★★★	1968 base engine convertibles
★★★★	1968 HO hardtops
★★★	1968 Base engine hardtops
★★★	1968 2bbl convertibles
★★	1968 2bbl hardtops
★★★★★	1969 Royal Bobcats
★★★★★	1969 Ram Air IV convertibles
★★★★★	1969 Judge convertibles
★★★★★	1969 Ram Air III convertibles
★★★★	1969 Ram Air IV hardtops
★★★★	1969 Ram Air III hardtops
★★★★	1969 Base engine convertibles
★★★	1969 Base engine hardtops
★★★	1969 2bbl convertibles
★★	1969 2bbl hardtops

The GTO received a totally redesigned body shell for 1968 that eliminated the box-atop-a-box design that had been prevalent in GM styling for almost fifteen years. The swoopy new body flowed the C-pillar into the rear quarter, and the lines were rounder and more bulging. The GTO looked muscular without a trace of fat.

Part of that redesign was a new bumper Pontiac had engineered in conjunction with Inland. Dubbed Endura, the urethane nose-piece was molded around a metal frame, allowing stylists to shape the front bumper in ways never done before. The Endura bumper could be painted to match the body color, and the GTO was the first GM car to receive this innovative new bumper. Pontiac took delight in airing commercials with a line of people waiting their turn to pound the energy-absorbing bumper with a crow bar. After taking a beating the bumper appeared none the worst for wear.

The new bumper completely surrounded and split the redesigned grilles in keeping with the traditional Pontiac theme. A Pontiac crest was mounted atop the center "beak" of the bumper. The headlamps were set horizontally, and a hidden headlamp option was available. For those not interested in a body-colored front bumper, the Le Mans chrome bumper was available, and 2,108 buyers chose it in 1968 (sixteen of them chose Ram Air-equipped cars). Beneath the bumper was a valance that rolled under the car with the parking lamps set in the corners of the panel.

The hood was broad and flat with twin scoops on either side of its centerline. These scoops were closed unless the Ram Air engine was ordered and the customer installed the open scoop ornaments. The hood also extended to the windshield, hiding the windshield wipers, another Pontiac first.

The flanks were remarkably clean and rounded. A bright panel covered the rockers, and the wheel openings were trimmed with bright moldings. The GTO emblem appeared in its usual location on the front fenders behind the wheel openings. At the rear of the quarter panels, a side marker lamp was shaped like the Pontiac crest and a GTO decal was placed in front of it. The massive chromed rear bumper incorporated the tail-lamps. The deck extended almost to the sloping rear window and ran down to the edge of the bumper. A smaller GTO nameplate appeared on the right-hand side of the decklid. Bright moldings trimmed the window openings and front and rear glass.

Both a convertible and hardtop were offered. New for 1968 was a shatterproof rear glass for the convertible. Part of the stunning new look was due to the fact that the wheelbase had been shortened by 3in, from 115 to 112. The chassis was still a perimeter design, with four-link rear, and unequal length upper and lower control arms up front. Coil springs were again used all around, but only the front received an antisway bar. Front disc brakes were again offered as an option.

The 1968 featured an entirely new body shell that sported a rounder body and a more muscular appearance. Pontiac designers purposely avoided the use of chrome trim to accentuate the GTO's clean styling.

1968 GTO Production

Body Style	Production	Engine	Trans
Hardtop	757	400 RA	Manual
Hardtop	183	400 RA	Auto
Hardtop	6,197	400 HO	Manual
Hardtop	3,140	400 HO	Auto
Hardtop	0	400 2bbl	Manual
Hardtop	2,841	400 2bbl	Auto
Hardtop	25,387	400 Std	Manual
Hardtop	39,215	400 Std	Automatic
Total Hardtop	77,704		

Convertible	92	400 RA	Manual
Convertible	22	400 RA	Auto
Convertible	766	400 HO	Manual
Convertible	461	400 HO	Auto
Convertible	0	400 2bbl	Manual
Convertible	432	400 2bbl	Auto
Convertible	3,116	400 Std	Manual
Convertible	5,091	400 Std	Auto
Total Convertible	9,980		

Total 1968 Production   87,684

The wheel base was reduced from 115in to 112in, giving the car a smaller look although overall length was similar to 1967. The C-pillar flowed into the quarter panels in one smooth curve. Notice the hood-mounted tachometer with which 5,931 GTOs were equipped in 1968.

1968 GTO Engine Codes

Engine Description	Engine Code	Comp. Ratio	HP
400 4bbl 3Spd Manual	WT	10.75:1	350
400 HO 3Spd Manual	WS	10.75:1	360
400 4bbl 4Spd	WT	10.75:1	350
400 HO 4Spd	WS	10.75:1	360
400 Ram Air Manual	XS	10.75:1	360
400 4BBl Automatic	YS	10.75:1	350
400 2bbl Automatic	XM	8.60:1	265
400 HO Automatic	YZ	10.75:1	360
400 Ram Air Automatic	XP	10.75:1	360

1968 GTO Transmission Codes

Six different transmissions were available for a 1968 GTO, the standard being a three-speed manual transmission with Hurst shifter. There were two choices of four-speed manual transmissions for 1968, a wide-ratio M20 four-speed was available for rear-end gear ratios up to 3.90:1. The other option was a close-ratio M21 four-speed available for cars equipped with 3.90:1 or 4.33:1* rear-end gear ratios. Three different Hydra-Matics were available for 1968, one for Ram Air cars, one for 2bbl cars only, and one for all other applications.

Transmission	Code
Three-Speed Manual Floor Shift	DB
Four-Speed Manual Wide-Ratio	FO
Four-Speed Manual Close-Ratio	FT
Hydra-Matic (2bbl Only)	PT
Hydra-Matic (Ram Air Only)	PQ
Hydra-Matic All Other Applications	PX

* There have been cases of close-ratio M21s ordered with higher axles.

1968 GTO Exterior Colors and Codes

Color	Code
Starlight Black	A
Cameo Ivory	C
Alpine Blue	D
Aegena Blue	E
Nordic Blue	F
April Gold	G
Autumn Bronze	I
Meridian Turquoise	K
Aleutian Blue	L

The front of the GTO was dominated by the Endura bumper. Hidden headlamps were optional. A valance panel rolled under the bumper and contained the parking lamps at each end.

Flambeau Burgundy	N
Springmist Green	P
Verdoro Green	Q
Solar Red	R
Primavera Beige	T
Nightshade Green	V
Mayfair Maize	Y

Convertible Top Colors and Codes

Color	Code
White	1
Black	2
Teal	5
Gold	8

Cordova Top Colors and Codes

Color	Code
Ivory	1
Black	2
Teal	5
Gold	8

The interior was also redone. The instrument panel was heavily padded, and a wood-grained panel ran the length of the dash from the instrumentation to the end of the glovebox. Three pods contained the instruments.

The Endura bumper was an engineering and styling breakthrough. It could tolerate a minor frontal impact and return to its original shape within twenty-four hours. Because it could be shaped in any contour, stylists were free to experiment with new front-end configurations and could paint the bumper to match the body.

Two Rally Gauge clusters were available in 1968, one with tachometer and one with clock. When a customer ordered a hood-mounted tachometer, he or she could also order the RPO 484 cluster with clock. The steering column and wheel were similar to 1967.

The optional console was heavily padded, and the Strato bucket seats received new upholstery. The door panels were also redone, and the door release handles were incorporated into the massive armrests, with the traditional GTO emblem just above.

The GTO's powertrains were carried over from 1967, starting with the optional, at no extra cost, two-barrel 265hp engine, again offered only with automatic transmission. The base 400ci engine was now rated at 350hp. The HO and Ram Air engines were rated at 360hp.

In March 1968, Pontiac released a new version of the Ram Air engine. Dubbed Ram Air II, it featured new heads with round exhaust ports, free-flowing exhaust manifolds, higher-lift camshaft, lighter-weight valves, special valve springs, larger push rods, forged-aluminum pistons with 10.75:1 compression, new crankshaft with tuned harmonic balancer, and a revised advance curve for the distributor. The Ram Air II was rated at 366hp at 5400rpm and 445lb-ft of torque at 3800rpm. It was the precursor to a new generation of Pontiac performance engines that would debut with the 1969 models.

For its exciting new styling, performance, and safety innovations, the 1968 GTO won the prestigious Motor Trend Car Of The Year award. Pontiac product planners projected 1968 to be a record-breaking year for the GTO with sales of over 100,000 because of its restyled body and Car Of The Year status. But all was not right for the GTO. The car was getting more expensive (the base price for the hardtop was $3,103; the convertible $3,327), and competitors such as Plymouth had attacked Pontiac's vulnerability by marketing the Road Runner, a bare bones musclecar that was standard with 383 engine, four-speed gearbox, and other features, for hundreds less.

1968 GTO Interior Colors and Codes

Color	Code
Turquoise	220
Gold	221
Black	223
Parchment	224
Red	225
Black	235*
Parchment	236*

* The bench seat option was again added to the regular line-up of interiors in 1968 with its own firewall ID number, making it easier to identify the bench seat interior. Bench seat interiors were offered in black or white.

Just in the event the buyer wasn't dazzled by the Endura bumper, he could order his 1968 GTO with the Le Mans chrome bumper. The Le Mans grilles were also used, but the GTO nameplate could be found in the left-hand grille.

1968 GTO Assembly Plant Codes

Code	Plant
A	Atlanta
B	Baltimore
G	Framingham
P	Pontiac
R	Arlington
Z	Fremont

When production ceased on August 2, 1968, and the final tallies were in, sales were up from 1967, reaching 87,684 units, but far short of projections. The musclecar market was continuing to heat up, and there were more choices for buyers than ever before. Pontiac knew it had to shake up the GTO's image, and it was ready with some surprises for 1969.

In keeping with an alternating cycle that saw styling changes one year and power-trains the next, the appearance of the 1969 GTO was quite similar to 1968. The front sheet metal was little changed, with revised parking lamps, new side marker lamps, new grilles, and the Pontiac crest removed from the bumper beak. The GTO nameplate still appeared in the left-hand grille on both exposed and hidden headlamps models.

The new hood used twin scoops with closed ornaments. When a buyer ordered a Ram Air engine, Pontiac installed a set of open scoops that fed cold air to the Rochester Quadra-Jet. It was considered a "fair weather" system in that water, leaves, and other debris could also be sucked down the scoops. It was up to the driver to reinstall the scoops when necessary.

1969 GTO Production

Body Style	Production	Engine	Trans
Hardtop		400 RA IV	Manual
Hardtop	151	400 RA IV	Auto
Hardtop	6,143	400 RA III	Manual
Hardtop	1,986	400 RA III	Auto
Hardtop	0	400 2bbl	Manual
Hardtop	1,246	400 2bbl	Auto
Hardtop	22,032	400 Std	Manual
Hardtop	32,744	400 Std	Auto
Hardtop Judge	6,725	NA	NA
Convertible	45	400 RA IV	Manual
Convertible	14	400 RA IV	Auto
Convertible	249	400 RA III	Manual
Convertible	113	400 RA III	Auto
Convertible	0	400 2bbl	Manual
Convertible	215	400 2bbl	Auto
Convertible	2,415	400 Std	Manual
Convertible	4,385	400 Std	Auto
Convertible Judge	108	NA	NA
Total Hardtop	58,126		
Total Convertible	7,328		
Total Judge Hardtop	6,725		
Total Judge Convert	108		
Total 1969 Production	72,287		

1969 GTO Engine Codes

Engine Description	Engine Code	Comp. Ratio	HP
400 4bbl 3Spd Manual	WT	10.75:1	350
400 RA III 3Spd Manual	WS	10.75:1	366
400 4bbl 4Spd	WT	10.75:1	350
400 RA III 4Spd	WS	10.75:1	366
400 Ram Air IV 4Spd	WW	10.75:1	370
400 4bbl Auto	YS	10.75:1	350
400 2bbl Auto	XX	8.60:1	265
400 RA III Auto	YZ	10.75:1	366
400 Ram Air IV Auto	XP	10.75:1	370

Cornering lamps were an usual option on 1968 GTOs. The wraparound parking lamps located in the valance panel met federal regulations for side marker lamps in 1968.

1969 GTO Transmissions

Six different transmissions were available for a 1969 GTO, the standard was a three-speed manual transmission with Hurst floor shifter. There were two choices of four-speed manual transmissions for 1969, a wide-ratio M20 four-speed was available for rear-end gear ratios up to 3.90:1. The other option was a close-ratio M21 four-speed available for cars equipped with 3.90:1 or 4.33:1* rear-end gear ratios. Three different Hydra-Matics were available for 1969, one for Ram Air cars, one for 2bbl cars only, and one for all other applications.

Transmission	Code
Three-Speed Manual Floor Shift	DB
Four-Speed Manual Wide-ratio	FO
Four-Speed Manual Close-ratio	FT
Hydra-Matic (2bbl Only)	PT
Hydra-Matic (Ram Air Only)	PQ
Hydra-Matic All Other Applications	PX

* There have been cases of close-ratio M21s ordered with higher axles.

1969 GTO Exterior Colors and Codes

Color	Number Code*	Letter Code
Starlight Black	10	A
Expresso Brown	61	B
Cameo White	50	C
Warwick Blue	53	D
Liberty Blue	51	E

Color	Number Code*	Letter Code
Winward Blue	87	F
Antique Gold	65	G
Limelight Green	59	H
Castillian Bronze	89	J
Crystal Turquoise	55	K
Claret Red	86	L
Midnight Green	57	M
Burgundy	67	N
Palladium Silver	69	P
Verdoro Green	73	Q
Matador Red	52	R
Champagne	63	S
Carousel Red	72	T
Nocturne Blue	88	V
Goldenrod Yellow	76	W
Mayfair Maize	40	Y

* Starting in 1969, the paint code on the cowl tag changed from a letter code to a number code.

Convertible Top Colors and Codes

Color	Code
White	1
Black	2
Dark Blue	3
Dark Green	9

Cordova Top Colors and Codes

Color	Code
Black	2
Dark Blue	3
Parchment	5
Dark Fawn	8
Dark Green	9

1969 GTO Interior Colors and Codes

Color	Code
Blue	250
Gold	252
Red	254
Green	256
Parchment	257
Black	258
Parchment	267*
Black	268*

* The bench seat option was again added to the regular line-up of interiors in 1969 with its own firewall ID number, making it easier to identify the bench seat interior. Bench seat interiors were offered in black and white.

This would be the last year for the GTO emblem that graced the fenders of every GTO built since 1964. As in years past, the field behind the GTO letters was finished in red, while the 6.5 litre designation and checkered motif below it were filled in with black.

Along the flanks, the GTO emblem used since 1964 was gone and was replaced by a GTO nameplate on the front fenders behind the wheel openings. At the rear of the quarter panels was a side marker lamp shaped in the diamond-style of the original GTO emblem. The rear bumper surrounded the taillamp bezels and the GTO nameplate appeared on the right rear of the decklid.

The instrument panel was again revised, with padding over the entire face of the instrument cluster. The three-pod design was still used to contain the gauges. Both versions of the Rally Gauge cluster were again offered. The standard wheel was a three-spoke design with center horn bar. The Custom Sports wheel was not as deep as previous years and sported a padded horn center cap. The igni-

1969 GTO Assembly Plant Codes

Code	Plant
A	Atlanta
B	Baltimore
G	Framingham
P	Pontiac
R	Arlington
Z	Fremont

tion switch was moved from the dash to the column, and an interlock system locked the transmission in park as well as the steering column to prevent theft.

Seat upholstery was redone, with a "Y" theme predominant in both the seat backs

The taillamps were incorporated in the massive rear bumper. Chrome exhaust extensions were offered at extra cost, as was the quarter-mounted power antenna.

At the rear of the quarter panels, a side marker lamp with jeweled lens was shaped in the Pontiac crest. In front of the lamp was a GTO decal, styled similarly to the GTO nameplates used in years past.

and the door panels. The GTO emblem on the door panel was new, as was the absence of vent windows. The console was similar to 1968, but when one ordered the optional console with automatic transmission, a new shifter was available (the Hurst Dual Gate was no longer offered) that still allowed the driver to shift gears or leave it in drive.

The standard 350hp engine could be replaced at no extra cost by the low-compression two-barrel version of the 400, rated at 265hp. The standard engine still featured chrome valve covers and dual snorkel air cleaner with chromed lid.

The next rung up the performance ladder was the new optional Ram Air engine (dubbed the Ram Air III). This engine could be easily identified when the hood was closed

The five-spoke Rally II road wheel had proven to be a popular option with GTO buyers. Red line G70x14 wide-tread tires were available. The Rally I wheel was also offered and was unchanged in appearance from 1966–1967.

1969 GTO Air Conditioning Production

Description	Production
Manual Transmission	
Hardtop	3,776
Convertible	330
Ram Air III convertible	22
Ram Air III hardtop	295
Automatic Transmission	
Ram Air III convertible	31
Ram Air III hardtop	729
Judge Ram Air III	787

Compiled by Fred Simmonds PMD

On hardtop models, the flowing C-pillar could create a blind spot when viewing rearward to make a lane change. The body is rounded and takes on the appearance of a fuselage. Note the lack of brightwork around the window glass. The only bright molding surrounds the back glass and roof gutter.

by the Ram Air decals on the outboard sides of the hood scoops. The Ram Air III used a flapper door arrangement with open scoops. The doors were activated by a cable control under the dash. The underhood system for the Ram Air consisted of a baffle bolted to the underside of the hood. A pan surrounded the carburetor and used a thick foam gasket that sealed against the underhood baffle when the hood was shut and the scoops were open. When the scoops were closed, warm underhood air was routed into the carburetor.

The Ram Air III was rated at 366hp and was available with three- or four-speed manual transmission or Turbo Hydra-Matic. Air conditioning was also offered with the Ram Air III, although the lowest rear gear ratio was limited to 3.23:1.

1969 Ram Air IV Production

Trans.	3.90:1 Gears	4.33:1 Gears
Four-speed	384	210
Automatic	127	38

Compiled by Fred Simmonds PMD

1969 Hood Tachometers
Used with Ram Air III and Ram Air IV

Description	Production
Ram Air III	3,439
Ram Air IV	271

Compiled by Fred Simmonds PMD

The top-performance engine for 1969 was the new Ram Air IV. Many of the components first released for the 1968 Ram Air II were found in the Ram Air IV, including round port exhausts, higher-lift hydraulic camshaft, stiff valve springs, special aluminum intake manifold, and exceptionally free-flowing exhaust manifolds. The Ram Air IV used the same air induction system as the Ram Air III, and it was grossly underrated at 370hp. Without doubt, the Ram Air IV was the finest street performance engine Pontiac had ever built.

Unlike the solid-lifter engines such as the Hemi and big-block Chevrolet, the Ram Air IV used hydraulic lifters and wasn't as finicky as other large-displacement performance engines. It was docile in traffic, didn't overheat, and didn't foul plugs. Only two rear axles

were offered with the Ram Air IV: 3.90:1 or 4.33:1 with the Ram Air IV. Mandatory options included heavy-duty radiator and Safe-T-Track limited-slip differential. A set of "Ram Air IV" decals were placed on the outboard sides of the hood scoops, announcing that this was the hottest of all GTOs.

Four transmissions were offered for 1969. A three-speed manual box with floor-mounted Hurst shifter was standard (not available with Ram Air IV). Two four-speeds, the wide-ratio M20 or close-ratio M21 were optional, both with Hurst shifters. The three-speed Turbo Hydra-Matic was the only available automatic transmission.

Pontiac had one more ace up its sleeve for 1969, and it played that card in December 1968 with the release of the GTO Judge. Although the Judge was originally conceived to

The instrument panel housed three pods containing all instrumentation. Shown here are air conditioning, Custom Sport wood wheel, stereo 8-track player, AM/FM radio, Rally Gauge cluster, and remote control outside driver's rearview mirror. The Hurst Dual Gate shifter was standard with automatic transmission.

The interior received some major changes in 1968, although the Strato bucket seats were carried over from 1967. The seats and door and quarter trim panels were recovered with new Morrokide upholstery. The optional center console was also heavily padded.

be a budget musclecar to compete with the Road Runner, by the time of its release it cost $332 more than the GTO. It was available in either a hardtop or convertible model.

Approximately the first 2,000 Judges were painted Carousel Red, a Firebird color not offered on the GTO. These cars had either white or black interiors. After February 20, 1969, the Judge was available in any GTO color. A wildly colored slash stripe adorned the upper beltline from the quarter window to the front bumper, and THE JUDGE decals were placed on the front fenders. The grilles were blacked out. Around back, a floating wing was bolted to the decklid and a smaller THE JUDGE decal was placed on the right top side of the wing. Rally II wheels were also standard, with the bright trim ring deleted. The interior was stock GTO, but a THE JUDGE emblem was tacked to the glovebox door (this emblem was delayed and was not installed on the first several thousand cars). Four-speed cars received a Hurst "T-Handle" instead of the usual shift ball.

The Judge was released as a spoof on the musclecar scene and was received poorly by enthusiasts. Instead of offering younger buyers a budget-priced GTO, the Judge was more expensive. The buyer had to be extremely extroverted or more than sure of his street racing ability, because other musclecar owners delighted in humbling the Judge at the stoplight drags. Whether it added to overall GTO sales is conjectural. Judge sales accounted for just under 10 percent of total 1969 GTO sales (6,833 out of 72,287 total production).

What to Look Out For

The new body shell for 1968–1969 had its share of rust problems. The area surrounding the rear window is prone to rust, as is the trailing edge of the decklid. The taillamp

The standard 400ci engine was rated at 350hp. Air conditioning was available with the 2bbl, standard, and HO engines. Note the single snorkel air cleaner with chromed lid. The valve covers were still chromed as part of the GTO package.

The Ram Air engine was rated at 360hp, thanks to a special camshaft and cold air induction system. In late February, the Ram Air II was released and was rated at 366hp.

The data plate was moved from the firewall to the left-hand side of the upper cowl, near the hood hinge. The VIN number was also moved from the door post to the left-hand top of the instrument panel and was visible through the base of the windshield.

On the assembly line at the Pontiac home plant, a 1968 GTO is being fitted with its Endura bumper. The valance panel was then installed. Notice that the GTO nameplate in the left-hand grille is slightly askew.

Styling changes were held to a minimum in 1969. The grilles were restyled, a GTO nameplate appeared on the front fenders behind the wheel openings, and a side marker lamp shaped was placed on the quarter panels. The 14x7 Rally II wheels were optional.

The only other body style offered in 1969 was the convertible. Note the massive chromed rear bumper and the GTO nameplate on the right rear of the decklid. A vinyl convertible top boot matched the interior color.

bezels are notorious for pitting, and trunk rust is also a common problem and can spread to the rear of the wheel openings. The Endura front bumper has always been plagued with paint adhesion problems, and it is nearly im-

possible to align the bumper properly to the hood and fenders.

On models with hidden headlamps, the actuators are vacuum activated. The vacuum canisters look like large tomato juice cans and

The Endura front bumper was little changed from 1968, except that the Pontiac crest was removed from the top of the bumper's "beak." Hidden headlamps were optional, as were the wire wheel covers.

New for 1969 was the Ram Air cold air induction system. The scoop ornaments were open and controlled by a flapper door that the driver could activate. When the doors were open, cold air was tamped into the carburetor. In the event of rain or snow, the doors were closed and only hot, under-hood air entered the carburetor. It was available on both the Ram Air III and Ram Air IV engines.

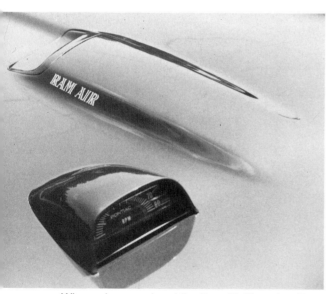

When a buyer ordered the Ram Air III engine, Pontiac installed this decal on the outboard sides of both hood scoops. The hood-mounted tachometer was an extra cost option on all GTOs and GTO Judges.

can spring leaks. The vacuum hoses throughout the system can also leak. Hoods tend to bend at the hood hinges, and rust-out of the fenders is not uncommon.

Interiors are generally durable, but the padded consoles are known to crack. The padded dash on the 1968–1969 GTO also cracks easily, and good replacements are hard to find. Piping on the seats also wears out, especially on the driver's seat. Check carefully around the rear window for water stains on the headliner and package shelf.

The big Kahuna of GTO engines in 1969 was the 370-horsepower Ram Air IV, a $558.20 option. When one ordered this engine, Pontiac installed special Ram Air IV decals on the outboard sides of the hood scoops. Only 759 1969 GTOs were equipped with the Ram Air IV engine.

The GTO's trunk was cavernous, but the spare tire consumed much of the space. The trunk area was finished off with a speckled or fleck finish. Look for bodywork inside the quarter panels and around the taillamps on these models.

This bench seat with four-speed gearbox is a very unusual combination. Note the standard steering wheel with tilt column and the unusual "Y" configuration of the door panel upholstery.

The optional Custom Sport steering wheel featured a padded center horn cap. The three pod theme for containing the instruments was carried over from 1968, but the instrument panel was redesigned. The stereo 8-track option was installed on the front of the console.

The center console was heavily padded and was prone to cracking. Note the Ram Air control under the dash and Hurst shifter with optional wood shift knob.

The Ram Air III—standard on the Judge package—was rated at 366hp, 16hp more the standard engine. It was available with air conditioning, but only with a 3.08:1 or 3.23:1 rear axle.

The Ram Air IV was rated at 370hp and featured round port exhausts, special exhaust manifolds, aluminum intake manifold, high-lift hydraulic camshaft, and other heavy-duty components. Only two rear axles were offered: 3.90:1 or 4.33:1.

The 1969 Judge has been one of the most counterfeited of all GTOs. There is no breakout in the VIN to identify the Judge option, and since the Judge is an option on the GTO, all it takes to create a bogus Judge is a repaint, stripes, blacking out the grilles, adding the proper interior and exterior emblems, replacing the shifter knob on manual transmission models, and bolting on a wing. Spotting a counterfeit Judge requires determined detective work. Documentation is still the best evidence. If the WT1 (Judge) option doesn't appear on the billing invoice, it's a fake. If a Ram Air III or Ram Air IV motor isn't installed, it's a fake. Since no Judges were built before January of 1969, a data plate with an earlier build date will prove it's a fake. The added weight of the wing required stiffer torque rods at the hood hinges to keep the decklid up when

The Judge was released in December 1968, but production did not begin until January 1969. The first several thousand Judges were painted Carousel Red, but beginning February 20, 1969, any GTO color was available. A slash stripe running along the upper beltline from the quarter window to the front fender was also part of the package. Its color combinations changed depending on exterior color.

open. Although not an empirical clue, the decklid shouldn't fall down on your head when opened. If it does, it may be a fake. Unless the car is painted Carousel Red and the date built code reads January or February, it may be a fake, since other colors in the GTO palette weren't offered on the Judge until later in the model year.

Best Buys

There are a host of best buys among the 1968 and 1969 GTOs. The Royal Bobcats were still available from Royal and are extremely rare today. Like any Bobcat, solid dealer documentation is required. Royal got out of the performance car market in 1969, and no Bobcats were built after that, although the Bobcat

As part of the Judge package, the grilles were blacked out, a large "The Judge" decal was placed on the front fenders, and the trim rings on the Rally II wheels were deleted. The Goodyear Eagle ST tires shown were not original equipment.

At the rear, a 60in wing was mounted to the deck-lid. Both convertible and hardtop Judges received this wing, but they are not interchangeable.

name and performance modification packages were sold through George DeLorean's Leader Automotive for several years after Royal closed out its program.

Best buys for 1968 are topped by the Ram Air II. Convertible models are the rarest, followed by hardtops. Ram Air convertibles and hardtops are next in line. Also desirable are the HO models in convertible and hardtop form. Standard engine convertibles are harder to find; hardtops are far more plentiful.

The 1969 Judge convertible is desirable, especially with a Ram Air IV engine (only five built). In fact, any Ram Air IV convertible (fifty-nine built) is worth its weight in gold

and will command top dollar. The Ram Air IV hardtop (700 built) is also an excellent investment. Judge hardtops with Ram Air IV engines (297 built) are priced slightly higher, depending on condition and documentation. Production of the Ram Air III engine was considerably higher (8,491 compared to the Ram Air IV at 759), so prices are somewhat lower for Judge and GTO hardtops. The standard engine convertible is a good investment, while standard engine hardtops are still widely available. The two-barrel engines in both 1968 and 1969 are not high-demand collectables and are not considered good investments.

The GTO's standard appearance package was included on the Judge, including the GTO nameplate on the decklid. Notice "The Judge" decal on the right-hand top side of the wing.

The Judge's interior was standard GTO, right down to the nylon twist carpet. Manual transmission-equipped Judges used a Hurst T-handle in place of the standard GTO shift ball and had a "The Judge" emblem on the glovebox door.

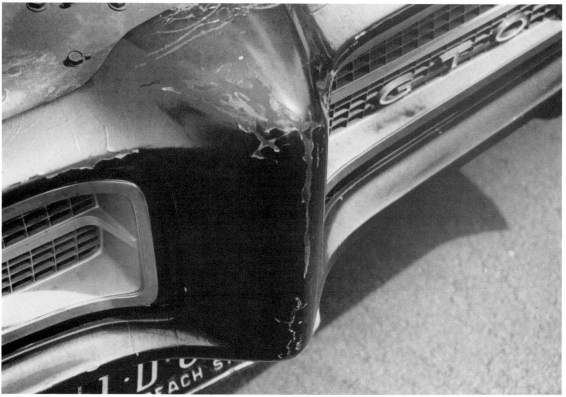

While the Endura urethane front bumper was hailed as an engineering and styling breakthrough, it turned out to be a maintenance headache. Paint adhesion was poor, and unless the proper flex agents were added to the paint when the car was resprayed, flaking and chipping was liable to occur soon after painting.

It's hard to believe one small glovebox emblem could elicit much controversy, but this one does. GTO Judge experts can't agree on when it was added to production. The supplier was unable to deliver the emblem on time when production began in January, and it is generally agreed that at least the first 2,000 Judges were not equipped with it.

Chapter 5

1970–1972 GTO

★★★★★	1970 Ram Air IV Judge convertibles
★★★★★	1970 Ram Air IV convertibles
★★★★★	1970 Ram Air III Judge convertibles
★★★★★	1970 Ram Air III convertibles
★★★★	1970 Ram Air IV Judge hardtops
★★★★	1970 Ram Air IV hardtops
★★★	1970 400/455 convertibles
★★★	1970 Ram Air III Judge hardtops
★★★	1970 Ram Air III hardtops
★★★	1970 400/455 hardtops
★★★★★	1971 Judge convertibles
★★★★★	1971 Judge hardtops
★★★★★	1971 455 HO convertibles
★★★★★	1971 400/455 convertibles
★★★★	1971 455 HO hardtops
★★★	1971 400/455 hardtops
★★★★★	1972 455 HO Ram Air sport coupes
★★★★★	1972 455 HO Ram Air hardtops
★★★★	1972 455 HO sport coupe
★★★★	1972 455 HO hardtops
★★★	1972 400/455 sport coupes
★★★	1972 400/455 hardtops

The 1970 GTO received something old and something new. The body styling was freshened with a new front end, revised flanks, and new tail. Up front, the Endura nose had been remolded with a more prominent snout and deeply recessed grilles that were blacked out with Argent Silver surrounds. The headlamps were frenched into the front with bright bezels. A valance panel rolled under with parking lamps located beneath the dual headlamps. A GTO nameplate was located in the left-hand grille.

The hood was basically unchanged from 1969. Along the sides, a distinctive bulge was molded in above the wheel openings. A scalloped corner lamp was located at the front of the fender, with a GTO nameplate decal located behind the front wheel opening.

Around back, the horizontal taillamps were incorporated into the bumper and wrapped around to serve as side marker lamps. A GTO nameplate appeared on the right rear of the decklid. Bright trim framed the drip moldings, the windshield, and back light. On convertible models, the rear window was made of solid tempered safety glass.

The interior was revised only slightly. The three-pod instrument panel design was essentially the same as in 1969, except for the imitation wood applique that covered the instrument panel housing. The switches and controls were placed under the gauges in a panel faced with an engine-turned applique. The hood-mounted tachometer was again offered, as were two versions of the Rally Gauge cluster (with or without clock). The seat upholstery featured a new "knitted" vinyl seat insert on the seat back and cushion. Head restraints were now standard, and the seatback release button was moved to the rear of the seat. A notch-back bench seat was also available. The door trim panels were restyled, with chrome-trimmed panels and a ribbed motif surrounding the armrest. A GTO nameplate emblem appeared above the armrest.

The 1970 GTO was the third installment of a styling cycle begun in 1968. The front was new from the cowl forward. Pontiac offered two body styles: hardtop and convertible.

The headlamps were frenched into the bumper and trimmed with bright bezels. The egg-crate grille and Argent Silver surrounds were deeply recessed into the bumper.

This preproduction photo shows the 1969 optional slash stripe applied to the 1970 GTO. Documented early production 1970 GTOs were built with this stripe. It was superseded by the D98 stripes above the wheel openings.

1970 GTO Production

Body Style	Production	Engine	Trans
Hardtop	627	400 RA IV	Manual
Hardtop	140	400 RA IV	Auto
Hardtop	3,054	400 RA III	Manual
Hardtop	1,302	400 RA III	Auto
Hardtop	1,761	455 4bbl	Manual
Hardtop	1,986	455 4bbl	Auto
Hardtop	9,348	400 Std	Manual
Hardtop	18,148	400 Std	Auto
Hardtop Judge	3,629	na	na
Convertible	24	400 RA IV	Manual
Convertible	13	400 RA IV	Auto
Convertible	174	400 RA III	Manual
Convertible	114	400 RA III	Auto
Convertible	158	455 4bbl	Manual
Convertible	241	455 4bbl	Auto
Convertible	887	400 Std	Manual
Convertible	2,173	400 Std	Auto
Convertible Judge	168	na	na
Total Hardtop	32,737		
Total Convertible	3,615		
Total Judge Hardtop	3,629		
Total Judge Convertible	168		
Total 1970 Production	40,149		

The GTO's Endura front end was restyled for 1970. The valance panel rolled beneath the bumper and contained the parking lamps and a narrow air inlet trimmed with a bright molding.

1970 GTO Engine Codes

Engine Description	Engine Code	Comp Ratio	HP
400 4bbl 3Spd Manual	WT	10.25	350
400 Ram Air III 3Spd Manual	WS	10.50	366
455 3Spd	WA	10.00	360
400 4bbl 4Spd	WT	10.50	350
400 Ram Air III 4Spd	WS	10.50	366
400 Ram Air IV 4Spd	WW	10.50	370
455 4Spd	WA	10.00	360
400 4bbl Automatic	YS	10.25	350
455 Automatic	YA	10.00	360
400 Ram Air III Automatic	YZ	10.50	366
400 Ram Air IV Automatic	XP	10.50	370

1970 GTO Transmission

Seven different transmissions were available for a 1970 GTO, the standard being a three-speed manual transmission with Hurst floor shifter. There were two choices of four-speed manual transmissions for 1970: a wide-ratio M-20 four-speed was available for rear-end gear ratios up to 3.90. The other option was a close-ratio M-21 four-speed available for cars equipped with 3.90 or 4.33* rear-end gear ratios. 455 cars had special four-speeds. Three different Hydra-Matics were available for 1970, one for Ram Air cars, one for 455 cars and one for all other 1970 GTO Applications.

Transmission	Code
Three-speed Manual Floor Shift	DG
Four-speed Manual Wide-Ratio	DJ
Four-speed Manual Close-Ratio	DL
Four-speed Manual 455	DP
Hydra-Matic (455 Only)	PR
Hydra-Matic (Ram Air Only)	PD
Hydra-Matic All Other Applications	PY

*There have been cases of close-ratio M-21S being ordered with higher axles.

The standard steering wheel was unchanged from 1969, and two optional wheels were offered, the three-spoke Custom Sports with padded horn button and the three-spoke Formula wheel with thickly padded rim and large horn button adorned with the Pontiac

Twin air scoops on the hood were functional when the Ram Air III or Ram Air IV engines were specified. They were also functional on the 455 engine option when Ram Air was ordered. This decal was used with the Ram Air III or the 455 with Ram Air.

crest. Consoles and shifters were largely unchanged from 1969.

A major change was in chassis and suspension. A rear antisway bar was added to the standard GTO four-link rear, and coil springs were now computer selected to improve ride and handling. Also new was variable ratio power steering, which changed the degree of power assist predicated on vehicle speed. The steering ratio was also revised downward from 15.0:1 to 12.4:1.

This decal was affixed to the scoops when the Ram Air IV engine was installed by the factory.

A GTO nameplate decal was located on the front fenders behind the wheel openings. If a buyer ordered the 455 engine option, the factory affixed a "GTO 455 CID" decal.

The instrument panel featured the three-pod design first used in 1968, but the panel face was covered in a wood-grained applique. An engine-turned applique faced the switch and control panel. The three-spoke Custom Sport steering wheel was optional.

Interior changes for 1970 included new seat upholstery that featured knitted vinyl seat inserts and new door and quarter trim panels. The three-spoke steering wheel was standard.

1970 GTO Exterior Colors and Codes

Color	Number Code	Letter Code
Starlight Black	19*	A
Palomino Copper	63	B
Polar White	10	C
Bermuda Blue	25	D
Atoll Blue	28	E
Lucerne Blue	26	F
Baja Gold	55	G
Palisade Green	45	H
Castillian Bronze	67	J
Mint Turquoise	34	K
Keylime Green	43	L
Pepper Green	48	M
Burgundy	78	N
Palladium Silver	14	P
Verdoro Green	47	Q
Cardinal Red	75	R
Coronado Gold	53	S
Orbit Orange	60	T
Carousel Red	65	V
Goldenrod Yellow	51	W
Sierra Yellow	50	Y
Granada Gold	58	Z

*Starting in 1969, the paint code on the cowl tag changed from a letter code to a number code.

Convertible Top Colors and Codes

Color	Code
White	1
Black	2
Sandalwood	5
Dark Gold	7

Cordova Top Colors and Codes

Color	Code
White	1
Black	2
Sandalwood	5
Dark Gold	7
Dark Green	9

The standard wheel for 1970 was a 14x6 stamped steel rim, covered with a bright hubcap. Optional were three wheel covers, the Deluxe, Custom, and Wire. The Rally II continued as the only optional sport road wheel. All GTOs were equipped with G70x14 tires

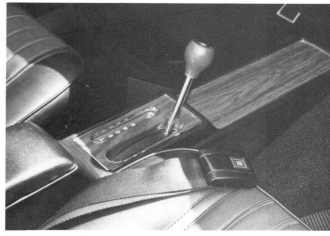

When a console was ordered with the M40 Turbo Hydra-Matic transmission, the shifter was moved from the column to the console. The shifter could either be placed in drive or could be up-shifted through the gears using a spring ratchet to prevent overrevving.

1970 GTO Interior Colors and Codes

Color	Code
Blue	250
Saddle	255
Green	256**
Sandalwood	257
Black	258
Black	253**
Red	254
Sandalwood	267*
Black	268*

*Denotes bench seat interior option.
**These colors were not available in 1970 GTO Convertibles.

1970 GTO Assembly Plant Codes

Code	Plant
A	Atlanta
B	Baltimore
G	Framingham
P	Pontiac
R	Arlington
Z	Fremont

from Goodyear, Firestone, or US Royal with either single or dual sidewall stripes or white lettered sidewalls.

The base engine displaced 400ci and was rated at 350hp. The twin-snorkel air cleaner had a chromed lid and the valve covers were also chromed.

The driver could activate the Ram Air cold air induction system by operating a knob under the dash. When the optional vacuum-operated exhaust was ordered (the VOE was offered only for a few months in the beginning of the model year), the knob was placed next to the Ram Air knob.

Drivetrains were essentially the same as in 1969 with two exceptions: the demise of the two-barrel engine and the addition of the 455ci engine, rated at 360hp. The 455 was available with both manual and automatic transmissions. Because of the increased torque (500lb-ft), all GTOs equipped with the 455 engine received 12-bolt rear axles. Only

two rear axle ratios were offered with the 455. The 3.31:1 was standard, and a 3.55:1 was optional. Those GTOs equipped with the 455 engine also had a "455 CID" decal placed below

When the scoops were opened, cold outside air was fed from the baffle attached to the underhood of the air cleaner.

A thick gasket surrounding the top of the air cleaner lid sealed against the baffle, preventing hot underhood air from entering the carburetor. This shot of cold air increased performance. This is the 366hp Ram Air III, which could be ordered with air conditioning. If you are considering buying a Ram Air GTO, make sure all the air induction components are intact, including the underhood baffle.

The top-performance engine was the Ram Air IV, rated at 370hp. It featured aluminum intake manifold, special round port heads, free-flowing exhaust manifolds, and higher lift hydraulic camshaft.

the GTO nameplate decal on the front fenders. The Ram Air option was available with the 455 engine.

The Judge option was carried over into 1970 and was again offered on hardtop and convertible models. The Judge was offered in any GTO color and received restyled stripes placed over the front and rear wheel openings. The hoodscoop bezels were painted flat black as were the grille surrounds, and a large wing stood above the rear decklid, attached to pedestals bolted to the decklid. "The Judge" decals appeared on the front fenders behind the wheel openings in place of the GTO nameplate decals, and another "The Judge" decal was placed on the right rear of the decklid, again displacing the standard GTO nameplate. A "The Judge" emblem was affixed to the glovebox door, and the Rally II wheel trim rings were deleted.

The Judge: Is It Or Isn't It?

While the variations in the Judge's appearance in 1970 could confuse even the most dedicated GTO restorer, the problem is compounded by the fact that some parts that were standard for the Judge could also be factory ordered for a standard GTO. For example, the rear wing was an option as were the side stripes (D98—also offered on Tempest and Le Mans). To make it even more perplexing, the Judge buyer could add trim rings to the Rally II wheels.

John Johnson of Mexico, Missouri, is one of the most noted Judge experts. He has been compiling data on the 1969–1971 Judge for almost twenty years and has developed some of the information printed here. He has also been surveying owners of Judges for pertinent information. If you want Judge information, you can contact John at 620 North Jefferson, Mexico, Missouri 65265.

All these components were standard as part of the Judge package, but variations appear to exist on these basic themes. For example, the Judge wing in 1970 was either painted black or body color and might have stripes on the sides of the wing that matched the style of the body stripes. Another variation was the installation or absence of a black fiberglass chin spoiler located below the valance panel. Buyers could also ignore the factory recommended body color and stripe usage combination and use their imagination in laying the wildest colored stripe on the most outrageous body color.

At the beginning of the model year, only the standard Ram Air III and the optional Ram Air IV engines were available for the Judge, but after November 25, the 455 was offered with only automatic transmission.

The GTO suffered along with the rest of the musclecar market in 1970. Sales dropped dramatically (down to 40,149 units) as the result of increased market competition, and some of that competition came from within Pontiac. The Trans Am, released in early 1970, featured a new body and Ram Air III and Ram Air IV engines.

A major blow to the musclecar market and the GTO was the move within the insurance industry to add surcharges onto high-performance cars' premiums. The industry had a "hit list" of musclecars that invoked ad-

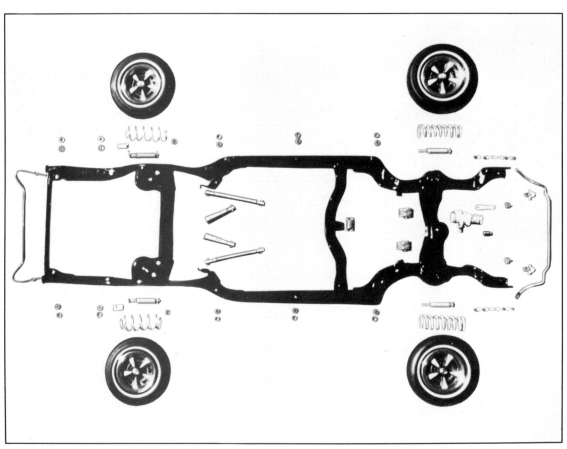

In 1970, the GTO suspension was revised and refined with the use of computer-selected springs and rear antisway bar. Variable ratio steering was also introduced, increasing power assist at low speeds and reducing it at high speeds. Spring and shock rates would continue to be tuned in 1971 and 1972, and antisway bar diameters would also be increased.

The Judge option was continued in 1970 and featured stripes over the wheel openings, blacked-out hood scoop bezels and grille surrounds, and Judge decals on the front fenders and rear decklid. The WT7 rear spoiler was either painted body color or was black on white cars (fifty-one produced).

ditional charges, and the young buying audience struggling to make the payments on a GTO now costing upwards of $4,000 was being priced out of the market by heavy insurance payments.

The market continued to dry up as the 1971 models were introduced. Pontiac chose to do only a facelift on the 1971, while they planned to give the 1972 A-body a complete makeover. A strike against GM forced the program to be moved back twelve months, consequently the basic body shell, introduced in 1968, was carried over into 1972. Since only small differences exist between the 1971 and 1972 GTOs, they are described together and the minor variations between the two years are noted where necessary.

Two body styles were offered in 1971, a hardtop coupe and convertible. In 1972, the GTO was demoted to option status on the Le Mans line up and was offered only as a hardtop coupe or sports coupe with B-pillar. The 1972 sports coupe does not feature hidden windshield wipers.

The Judge was offered in a convertible was well as
hardtop. Note the absence of trim rings on the Rally
II wheels, standard as part of the Judge package.

1971 GTO Production Figures

Body Style	Production	Engine	Trans
Hardtop	476	455 HO	Manual
Hardtop	412	455 HO	Auto
Hardtop	0	455 4bbl	Manual
Hardtop	534	455 4bbl	Auto
Hardtop	2,011	400 Std	Manual
Hardtop	6,421	400 Std	Auto
Total Hardtop	9,854		
Convertible	21	455 HO	Manual
Convertible	27	455 HO	Auto
Convertible	0	455 4bbl	Manual
Convertible	43	455 4bbl	Auto
Convertible	79	400 Std	Manual
Convertible	508	400 Std	Auto
Total Convertible	678		
Total Production	10,532		

Hardtop	9,497	NA	NA
Hardtop Judge	357	NA	NA
Convertible	661	NA	NA
Convertible Judge	17	NA	NA
Total Judge	374		
Total Production	10,532		

The GTO and the Judge were at home on the drag strip. Many owners of GTOs enjoy drag racing their GTOs as well as participating in concours events.

Is it or isn't it? Although this GTO is wearing a Judge license plate, it could just be dressed out with some of the Judge options, such as the WT7 rear wing or the D98 stripes. This particular GTO also has the optional hood-mounted tachometer.

The Judge interior is identical to the standard GTO cockpit with the exception of a "The Judge" emblem attached to the glovebox door. Note placement of Ram Air knob under the dash.

1971 GTO Engine Codes

Engine Description	Engine Code	Comp. Ratio	HP
400 4bbl 3Spd Manual	WT	8.20	300
400 4bbl 4Spd Manual	WK	8.20	300
455 HO 3Spd*	WL	8.40	335
455 HO 4Spd*	WC	8.40	335
400 Auto	YS	8.20	300
455 4bbl Auto	YC	8.20	325
455 HO Auto*	YE	8.40	335

* A Ram Air system was available with the 455 HO motor.

When equipped with manual transmission, the shifter (all manual transmission-equipped GTOs used Hurst shifters) was topped with a Hurst T-handle. Note the location of the optional 8-track stereo on the console.

1971 GTO Transmission Codes

Six different transmissions were available for a 1971 GTO, the standard being a three-speed manual transmission with heavy-duty floor shifter. There were two choices of four-speed manual transmissions for 1971, including a wide-ratio M20 four-speed and a close-ratio M-22 four-speed, also known as a "Rock Crusher." Three different Hydra-Matics were available for 1971, one for all 400 4bbl cars, one for 455 cars, and one for 455 HO GTOs.

Transmission	Letter Code
Three-Speed Manual Floor Shift	RM
Four-Speed Manual Wide-ratio	WT
Four-Speed Manual Close-ratio (M-22)	WO
400 4bbl Automatic	PX
Hydra-Matic (455 Only]	PW
Hydra-Matic 455 HO	PQ

1971 GTO Exterior Colors and Codes

Color	Number Code	Letter Code
Starlight Black	19*	A
Sandalwood	61	B
Cameo Ivory	11	C
Adriatic Blue	24	D
Lucerne Blue	26	F
Limekist Green	42	H

The GTO hardtop for 1971 had a restyled front end. The Endura front bumper was redesigned and the grille openings enlarged.

Tropical Lime	43	L
Laurentian Green	49	M
Nordic Silver	13	P
Cardinal Red	75	R
Castillian Bronze	67	S
Canyon Copper	62	T
Quezal Gold	53	Y
Aztec Gold	59	Z

* Starting in 1969, the paint code on the cowl tag changed from a letter code to a number code.

Convertible Top Colors and Codes

Color	Code
White	1
Black	2
Sandalwood	5
Dark Brown	7
Dark Green	9

Cordova Top Colors and Codes

Color	Code
White	1
Black	2
Sandalwood	5
Dark Green	9

The front end was facelifted for 1971–1972. The Endura bumper was restyled and the headlamps were now above the main bumper bar and trimmed with bright bezels. The grilles had a cross-hatch design in 1971 and were only slightly recessed. The 1972 blacked-out grilles were egg-crate and deeply recessed with Argent Silver surrounds. Large round parking lamps appeared below the bumper bar on the outer ends of the lower valance, with a cross-hair design in the 1972

The GTO convertible entered its last year of production in 1971. The sides and rear bumper are virtually unchanged from 1970, with the rear lamps wrapping around to serve as side markers. Note dual exhaust tips that exit under the bumper.

The dual headlamps were not integrated into the bumper as in previous years. The hood was also restyled, and the scoops were moved forward and enlarged. The crosshatch grilles were slightly recessed.

lamp lens. A GTO nameplate appeared in the LH grille.

The hood had a large pair of scoops that were open and not controlled by the driver. If a Ram Air engine was ordered, "Ram Air" decals were placed on the outboard sides of the scoops. Along the sides, twin horizontal side lamps are located directly behind the front bumper. The flanks of the 1971 and 1972 are nearly identical to the 1970 GTO, with a nameplate decal on the front fenders behind the wheel openings on 1971 models. The 1972 GTO sports a functional air extractor behind the front wheel opening, moving the GTO decal to the rear quarter panel. When the 455 HO was ordered in 1972, the "455 HO" decal appeared under the GTO decal on the quarter panel. Around back, the rear bumper and wraparound taillamp theme was retained, but the rear lamp lenses were slightly different.

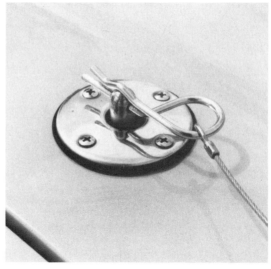

Hood pins were offered in 1971 and used plastic-coated cables to prevent them from being lost.

1971 GTO Interior Colors and Codes

Color	Code
Blue	261
Ivory	262
Saddle	256**
Sienna	264
Jade	266**
Sandalwood	267**
Black	269
Sandalwood	277*
Black	279*

* Denotes bench seat interior option.
** These colors were not available in 1971 GTO convertibles.

When the GTO was equipped with Ram Air cold air induction, decals were placed on the outboard sides of the scoops.

Depending on engine installation, either "GTO" or "GTO 455 CID" decals were placed on the front fenders behind the wheel openings.

Two sport road wheels were offered in 1971, the Rally II and the Honeycomb (shown). Both wheels were offered in 14in and 15in diameters.

The 1971 Ram Air system was comprised of open scoops on the hood, which fed air to two "boots" that fitted to a baffle attached to the underhood. When buying a Ram Air-equipped GTO, make sure this assembly is in place.

1971 GTO Assembly Plant Codes

Code	Plant
A	Atlanta
B	Baltimore
G	Framingham
P	Pontiac
R	Arlington
Z	Fremont

Body-colored outside rear-view sport mirrors were new for 1971.

Inside, the upholstery patterns were changed for 1971, as were the door panels, which featured an insert framed by twin bright moldings encompassing the window crank and armrest. The instrument panel was identical to the 1970 design, except the wood-style veneer was replaced with a pebble-grained fascia and the alpha numerics of the gauges are shorter and thicker in appearance. The stereo cassette player, which mounted on the console under the instrument panel, was a new option. It was canceled early in the production year.

Since the 1972 GTO was now a Le Mans option, the interior came in two trim levels—Le Mans and Le Mans sport. The Le Mans interior was standard with a cloth and vinyl bench seat and full-length rubber floor mats. In hardtop coupes, the rubber floor mat was replaced with nylon loop pile carpeting. The Morrokide all-vinyl bench seat with nine vertical ribs on the cushion and seat back was optional. The door panel upholstery was the same on both levels of interior trim. The optional Le Mans sport interior featured Strato Bucket seats and padded door panels with pull strap and carpeting trimming the lower portion of the panel.

On 1972 GTOs, the instrument panel was virtually unchanged from 1971 except for a teakwood applique around the instrument pods and the name "PONTIAC" embossed into the dash pad above the right corner of the glovebox door. The speedometer was reduced from 140 to 120mph and a seatbelt warning lamp appeared in the speedometer face. A two-spoke steering wheel was standard with the horn buttons in each spoke. The Formula wheel was still offered optionally.

The 455 HO with Ram Air used this air cleaner with openings in the tops of the twin snorkels that fitted to the "boots" attached to the underhood baffle.

1972 GTO Production Figures

Body Style	Production	Engine	Transmission
Coupe	3	455 HO	Manual
Coupe	7	455 HO	Auto
Coupe	0	455 4bbl	Manual
Coupe	5	455 4bbl	Auto
Coupe	59	400 Std	Manual
Coupe	60	400 Std	Auto
Total Coupe	134		
Hardtop	310	455 HO	Manual
Hardtop	325	455 HO	Auto
Hardtop	0	455 4bbl	Manual
Hardtop	235	455 4bbl	Auto
Hardtop	1,519	400 Std	Manual
Hardtop	3,284	400 Std	Auto
Total Hardtop	5,673		
Total 1972 Production	5,807		

The 455 HO could also be ordered without the Ram Air option. It used a standard air cleaner with open front snorkels. All 1971 GTO engines came with black-painted air cleaners and valve covers that matched the engine color.

1972 GTO Engine Codes

Engine Description	Engine Code	Comp. Ratio	HP
400 4bbl 3Spd Manual	WS	8.20	250
400 4bbl 4Spd Manual	WK	8.20	250
455 HO 4Spd *	WM	8.40	300
400 Automatic	YT	8.20	250
455 4bbl Automatic	YK	8.20	250
455 HO Automatic*	YB	8.40	300

* A Ram Air system was available with the 455 HO motor.

The standard gauge package featured a fuel gauge in the left pod with telltale lamps for oil pressure, water temperature, and volts. The right-hand pod was either blank or fitted with the optional clock. Notice the automatic shifter placement on the column when the center console was not ordered.

The 1971 interior was little changed from 1970 with the exception of the panel surrounding the gauges, which was now covered with a grained vinyl. The door and quarter trim panels were redesigned, as was the seat upholstery. The center console was an extra cost item.

1972 GTO Transmission Codes

Six different transmissions were available for a 1972 GTO, the standard was a three-speed manual transmission with heavy-duty floor shifter. There were two choices of four-speed manual transmissions for 1972, including a wide-ratio M20 four-speed and a close-ratio M-22 four-speed, also known as a "Rock Crusher." Three different Hydra-Matics were available for 1972, one for all 400 4bbl cars, one for 455 cars, and one for 455 HO GTOs.

Transmission	Code
Three-Speed Manual Floor Shift	RM
Four-Speed Manual Wide-ratio	WT
Four-Speed Manual Close-ratio (M-22)	WO
400 4bbl Automatic	PX
Hydra-Matic (455 Only]	PR
Hydra-Matic 455 HO	PQ

The biggest change from 1970 was under the hood. The engine line-up was reduced, although a new version of the 455 was available, and all engines suffered a drop in horse-power. This was due to a reduction in compression and a switch to rating horsepower by the net instead of gross SAE method. With manual transmissions, only the 400ci engine rated at 300hp and the new 455 HO, rated at 335hp, were offered. With the three-speed Turbo Hydra-Matic, the 400, a 325hp version of the 455, and the 455 HO were available.

The 1971 GTO door panel had a center section highlighted with a twin bright moldings. A GTO emblem appeared above the armrest. Note the remote control for the outside rearview mirror.

With its blacked-out grilles and aggressive Endura front nose, the 1971 Judge entered its last year of production. The 455 HO was the only engine offered with the Judge. While dismal sales caused it to be pulled before the end of the model year, today the 1971 Judge is one of the most collectible of all GTOs.

1972 GTO Exterior Colors and Codes

Color	Number Code	Letter Code
Cameo Ivory	11*	C
Adriatic Blue	24	D
Quezal Gold	53	E
Lucern Blue	26	F
Brittany Beige	50	G
Shadow Gold	55	H
Brasillia Gold	57	J
Springfield Green	43	L
Wilderness Green	48	M
Revere Silver	14	N
Cardinal Red	75	R
Anaconda Gold	63	S
Monarch Yellow	56	Y
Sundance Orange	65	Z

Convertible Top Colors and Codes

The convertible option was dropped in 1972.

Cordova Top Colors and Codes

Color	Code
White	1
Black	2
Pewter	4
Beige	6
Tan	7

* Starting in 1969, the paint code on the cowl tag changed from a letter code to a number code.

The side stripes, decals, and rear wing used on the 1971 are identical to those used on the 1970 Judge. While dechromed Rally II wheels were a standard part of the Judge package, Honeycomb wheels could be specified as an extra cost option. Only 374 Judges were built in 1971: 357 hardtops and seventeen convertibles.

The 455 HO picked up where the Ram Air IV left off. It retained the RA IV's aluminum intake, round port exhaust heads, and free-flowing exhaust manifolds. The black air cleaner (the valve covers were no longer chromed but painted Pontiac Engine Blue) sported a large "455 HO" air cleaner. If the buyer ordered the optional Ram Air, twin boots were installed on the underside of the hood that mated to large openings in the air cleaner's twin snorkels that funneled cold air to the Rochester Quadra-Jet. This setup was also available on the 400 engine. The Ram Air system was a full-time air induction system controlled by water temperature and manifold vacuum to actuate flapper doors in the air cleaner. A series of baffles and drains in the scoops prevented rain and debris from getting into the system.

A "The Judge" decal replaced the GTO nameplate on the rear decklid. The "455 HO" decal was placed on the ends of the rear wing. The wing was painted body color, but UPC WT7-604 allowed buyers of Cameo White Judges to specify a black wing. Only fifteen buyers took advantage of this option.

The Judge could be loaded with options, like the interior of this '71 was. Along with the Custom Sport steering wheel, this Judge sports remote driver's side outside rearview mirror, stereo 8-track, AM/FM radio, and air conditioning (150 1971 Judges were equipped with air conditioning). Note the Hurst T-handle and "The Judge" glovebox door emblem, both standard parts of the Judge.

1972 GTO Interior Colors and Codes

Color	Code
Blue	241*
Green	244*
Beige	245*
Saddle	253**
Green	254**
White	252**
Black	256**
Green	274***
White	272***
Black	276***
Pewter	270***

* Denotes cloth & vinyl bench seat interior option.
** Optional Morrokide bench seat interior.
*** Optional expanded Morrokide strato bucket seat interior.

1972 GTO Assembly Plant Codes

Code	Plant
A	Atlanta
B	Baltimore
G	Framingham
P	Pontiac
R	Arlington
Z	Fremont

The transmission lineup consisted of the M13 three-speed manual gearbox, the M20 and M22 four-speed transmissions (the M22 was standard with the 455 HO), and the M40 Turbo Hydra-Matic. Rear gears in the 455 HO line-up were limited to a lowest of 3.55:1, while the 400 could be ordered with up to a 4.33:1 ratio with the M22 Rock Crusher.

The 1972 GTO reverted back to option status on both the Le Mans and Le Mans sport packages, and only minor changes were made. The grilles were restyled with an egg-crate design and re-cessed deeper into the bumper. This preproduction 1972 uses the 1971-style parking lamps. The correct 1972 lamp lenses have a crosshairs design.

The 1972 engine line-up was virtually unchanged from 1971, but engine horsepower was now strictly calculated by SAE net, reducing the output of the standard 400 and the optional 455 (automatic transmission only) engines to 250hp. The 455 HO was whittled back to 300hp net. The Ram Air induction system was still offered.

Two optional wheel covers were offered in 1971, the Custom wheel disc and the Wire wheel disc. Joining the Rally II was a new sport road wheel, the Honeycomb, so named for its hexagon-shaped blocks that made up the shape of the rim. Wheels were now offered in 14in or 15in diameters. Whitewalls or white-lettered tires were available.

The Judge entered it final year of production in 1971. It came standard with the 455 HO engine with Ram Air, three-speed manual transmission, dechromed Rally II wheels, blacked-out grilles, rear deck air foil (optional black on white cars), Judge stripes and decals, and a "The Judge" emblem on the glovebox door.

The Judge stripes were the same as 1970, and the grilles were blacked out. The rear wing sported "455 HO" decals on the outboard sides of the wing, since a "The Judge" decal replaced the GTO and 455 HO engine displacement decals on the front fenders. The Judge interior was standard GTO and was offered with all GTO options and accessories. On manual transmission models, a Hurst "T-Handle" was used on the shifter.

Sales of the 1971 Judge were not encouraging, and production was halted in January

Two body styles were offered in 1972, the hardtop coupe (shown) and the sports coupe with B-pillar (offered only on the base Le Mans package). Placement of trim is identical to 1971.

The Endura front nose was standard as part of the GTO option. Argent Silver surrounds frame the blacked-out grilles and a GTO nameplate appears in the left-hand grille. The Endura bumper was always difficult to align to the hood and fenders. Note correct crosshairs parking lamps lens.

of 1971 after only 357 hardtops and seventeen convertibles were built.

Sales continued to slide at an alarming rate in the early seventies. The 1971 GTO registered sales of only 10,532 units, and the 1972 model's performance was even worse, tallying only 5,807 GTOs built and sold. The glory days for the GTO were over.

What to Look For

Many of the rust problem areas of the 1969 GTO are prevalent in the 1970–1972 models. The rear window surround was prone to rust out, with trunk rust out resulting from water entering through rusted holes around the back glass. This rust out was usually caused by the piercings in the metal to retain the bright moldings. Water would seep in under the moldings and eat away at the metal. Rust along the lower beltline from the front fenders to the rear quarters is common, as are rusted out decklids due to poor drainage.

The painted Endura bumpers fade faster than the steel hood and fenders, resulting in paint mismatch. The fit on the 1970 Endura bumper is often poor, although the 1971–1972 models are somewhat better. Check for hoods that are slightly bent at the hinges and rust in the 1971–1972 underhood. Windshield wiper problems also crop up on these cars.

Interior problems center around the dash pads, which are prone to cracking and splitting, as are the padded consoles. Water leakage from the lower front windshield can cause damage to the passenger side carpet and floorpan. Heater cores are also prone to failure, and a bum core will pour coolant all over the console and carpet. Heater core replacements are the bane of the GTO owner because the core is buried in the firewall, and in air-conditioned models they're a nightmare to access and replace.

You cannot easily verify a Judge or Ram Air IV GTO without paperwork and documentation. Beware of window stickers, because they can be forged thanks to reproduction stickers available from vendors. A billing invoice from Pontiac Historical Services is essential here, since these particular cars can command prices above $22,000. There is no distinction in the VIN or data plate to identify a Ram Air IV or Judge, so look for heavy-duty components in Ram Air IV models such as the Code 621 Firm Ride and Handling Package with heavier duty antisway bar and 3.90:1 or 4.33:1 rear axle. Also, air conditioning was not offered with Ram Air IV GTOs.

Best Buys

When it comes to the best buys in the 1970 GTO model lineup, The Judge convertible (162 built) is the most desirable, followed by Ram Air IV convertibles (thirty-seven built) and hardtops (767 built). The Judge was standard with the Ram Air III engine, and both hardtops and convertibles are solid investments, with Orbit Orange versions worth slightly more. Ram Air III convertibles and hardtops are also good buys and will enjoy a solid appreciation in the coming years. Base

Only the 1972 GTO (and Le Mans sport with the optional Endura front end) received these functional air extractors located behind the wheel openings in the front fenders.

The base engine was the 400ci powerplant rated at 250hp. The 455 was offered with M40 Turbo Hydra-Matic and was also rated at 250hp. The top engine option was again the 455 HO, pegged at 300hp and offered with manual or automatic transmissions. The absolute lowest rear axle ratio was 3.55:1 (air conditioning not available). All rears with 455 HO applications used an 8.88in ring gear.

engine GTOs are always in demand. Look for models equipped with unusual options such as hood tach, vacuum-operated exhaust (produced in limited numbers early in the model year), and loaded versions with air conditioning and all power options.

The optional three-spoke Formula steering wheel was introduced in 1970. It was available only with power steering. Cruise control, tilt column, air conditioning, and stereo 8-track player mounted on the console were all popular 1972 options.

The top interior package included padded door panels with pull handles. Although styled very similar to the 1971 GTO door panels, there were no GTO emblems on the 1972 panels.

Some of the best buys in the GTO hobby can be found among the 1971–1972 models. Although they lost favor with enthusiasts because of reduced compression ratios and lower horsepower ratings, these GTOs boast the stump-pulling 455 HO, a tremendous engine that came in some rather unusual combinations. For example, all 1971 GTO Judges were equipped with the 455 HO engine (only seventeen 1971 Judge convertibles were built, and they are extremely desirable). There were also only forty-eight 455 HO GTO convertibles built in 1971, making them also a best buy for the GTO enthusiast. The 455 HO hardtop is also a guaranteed winner, and because 1971 was the last year for the soft top, any 1971 convertible is an above-average investment.

Things get rather murky when it comes to identifying the 1972 GTO because it was an option (UPC W62) on the Le Mans coupe and Le Mans Sport hardtop and convertible. Unlike the 1966–1971 models, the 1972 has no "242" designator in the VIN, although the engine code was incorporated into the VIN. The fifth character is a letter indicating engine displacement. The base engine is identified by the letter "T"; the 455 engine option is "Y"; and the 455 HO is "X." Checking this code against the engine in the cradle is a good way to spot counterfeits.

When inspecting a 1972 GTO, remember that no factory records verify the building of a 1972 GTO convertible. Because of public demand, many dealers took 1972 Le Mans sports convertibles (the Le Mans Sport came with the optional Endura front end) and dressed them out to look like GTO convertibles. To muddy the waters even further, the 455 HO was offered in both the Le Mans Sport hardtop and convertible, as well as the Le Mans coupe. There were some rare and verified combinations of GTO 455 HO applications, including such nuggets as three M22 four-speed and seven M40 Turbo Hydra-Matic 455 HO Le Mans coupes with the GTO option. Once again, a billing invoice is essential to substantiate the car's pedigree.

The WW5 package was offered in 1972 and combined all the best attributes Pontiac had to offer on the GTO. It included the code 34X 455 HO engine, choice of four-speed or automatic transmission, limited-slip rear,

Cordova tops were optional on all 1970–1972 GTOs. The edges of the top are trimmed with bright moldings along the A-pillars and the bottom of the C-pillars.

Ram Air was again available and was standard as part of the WW5 package, as indicated by the Ram Air decals on the outboard sides of the hood scoops. The rear wing was also offered as an option.

Prior to production, a "ducktail" spoiler was planned as an option for the 1972 GTO. Although the option was canceled, a few GTOs received the spoiler. It was also planned as an over-the-counter package, and a few of those were also sold. A 1972 GTO with this spoiler would be an excellent investment.

All 1972 GTOs were equipped with exhaust splitters reminiscent of the 1964–1965 tips. They exited just behind the rear wheels.

body-colored outside mirrors, Formula steering wheel, roof drip scalp moldings, power front disc brakes, custom carpets, Rally Gauge cluster with tachometer, and handling package. The 1972 GTO with the WW5 option was one of the finest road cars Pontiac would build, combining brutal performance, superb handling, excellent braking response, and luxurious comfort. Only three were built on the Le Mans coupe platform and 287 on the Le Mans sport. It is the most desirable of all the 1972 GTOs.

The 455 and base 400 engines are far behind the 455 HO in value and collectibility, but examples of these two equipped with a brace of luxury options can still command decent prices and make great weekend drivers. With low production (5,807 total units built), they still have potential to appreciate. Choosing the most desirable 1972 GTO is still affordable and will prove to be a worthwhile investment in the years to come.

The 1972 GTO interior was offered in three levels of trim. The base Le Mans interior featured a cloth and vinyl bench seat and specific door and quarter trim panels. The next step up was an all-Morrokide bench seat with full carpeting. Top interior trim level included Strato bucket seats. The word "Pontiac" is embossed in the dash pad just above the glovebox door. The underdash tape deck shown here is an aftermarket unit.

Chapter 6

1973– 1974 GTO

★★	**1973 455 coupes**
★★	**1973 400 coupes**
★	**1973 455 sport coupes**
★	**1973 400 sport coupes**
★★	**1974 Hatchback**
★	**1974 Notchback**

In 1970, the management team that had nurtured Pontiac through the sixties was replaced by new leadership, and its interpretation of the Pontiac product line-up was self-evident by 1973. The GTO's fortunes continued to decline while the Trans Am took center stage as the division's performance star.

Sharing the new A-body with the GTO was the Grand Am, a European-inspired luxury sports coupe/sedan that wore a new Endura front end, was shod with sophisticated suspension, and boasted luxurious interior appointments. The Grand Am was everything the GTO should have been.

The 1973 GTO wore new sheet metal and was offered as an option on the Le Mans and Le Mans sport coupe (shown). Standard wheel covers were the baby moons and trim rings, with Deluxe and Finned wheel covers optional. Two road wheels were also optional, the Rally II and the Honeycomb. All GTOs were equipped with G60x15 tires.

Twin NACA-style air ducts were placed at the top of the hood. The scoops were nonfunctional, but the lower scoop cover could be removed to increase performance slightly.

The top GTO interior for 1973 featured bucket seats covered in all vinyl Morrokide. A wood-grained panel trimmed the glovebox door. On the door panels, a GTO nameplate appeared above the armrest.

1973 GTO Production Figures

Body Style	Production	Engine	Trans
Coupe	0	455 4bbl	Manual
Coupe	25	455 4bbl	Auto
Coupe	187	400 4bbl	Manual
Coupe	282	400 4bbl	Auto
Total Coupe	494		
Sport Coupe	0	455 4bbl	Manual
Sport Coupe	519	455 4bbl	Auto
Sport Coupe	926	400 4bbl	Manual
Sport Coupe	2,867	400 4bbl	Auto
Total Sport Coupe	4,312		
Total Production	4,806		
Coupe	0	455 4bbl	Manual
Coupe	25	455 4bbl	Auto
Coupe	187	400 4bbl	Manual
Coupe	282	400 4bbl	Auto
Total Coupe	494		
Sport Coupe	0	455 4bbl	Manual
Sport Coupe	519	455 4bbl	Auto
Sport Coupe	926	400 4bbl	Manual
Sport Coupe	2,867	400 4bbl	Auto
Total Sport Coupe	4,312		
Total 1973 Production	4,806		

1973 GTO Early Production Engine Codes

Description	Letter ID	UPC
400 4bbl w/3-Spd Trans	WS	L78
400 4bbl w/3-Spd Trans*	WK	L78
400 4bbl w/4-Spd Trans	WP	L78
400 4bbl w/Hydra-Matic	YS	L78
400 4bbl w/Hydra-Matic**	ZS	L78
400 4bbl w/Hydra-Matic*	YY	L78
400 4bbl w/Hydra-Matic*	Y3	L78
400 4bbl w/Hydra-Matic***	YT	L78
455 4bbl w/Hydra-Matic	YC	L75
455 4bbl w/Hydra-Matic**	ZC	L75
455 4bbl w/Hydra-Matic*	YA	L75
455 4bbl w/Hydra-Matic**	ZA	L75
455 4bbl w/Hydra-Matic***	YK	L75
455 4bbl w/Hydra-Matic*	YD	L75

1973 GTO Late Production Engine Codes

Description	Letter ID	UPC
400 4bbl w/3-Spd Trans	YF	L78
400 4bbl w/4-Spd Trans	Y6	L78
400 4bbl w/4-Spd Trans*	YG	L78
400 4bbl w/Hydra-Matic	XN	L78
400 4bbl w/Hydra-Matic*	XX	L78
400 4bbl w/Hydra-Matic**	XK	L78
455 4bbl w/Hydra-Matic	XE	L75
455 4bbl w/Hydra-Matic*	XL	L75
455 4bbl w/Hydra-Matic**	X7	L75
455 4bbl w/Hydra-Matic***	XM	L75

* Cars equipped with unitized ignition.
** High-country use.
*** High-country use equipped with unitized ignition.

1973 GTO Early Production Transmission Codes

Description	Letter ID	UPC
Three-Speed Manual Trans	TD	M13
Four-Speed Manual Trans	UA	M20
Hydra-Matic w/400 4bbl	PG	M40
Hydra-Matic w/455 4bbl	PR	M40

1973 GTO Late Production Transmission Codes

Description	Letter ID	UPC
Three-Speed Manual Trans	RM	M13
Four-Speed Manual Trans	WD	M20
Hydra-Matic w/400 4bbl	P2G	M40
Hydra-Matic w/455 4bbl	P2R	M40

The new A-body shell was controversial in appearance, and as a GTO (still an option on the Le Mans), it left a lot to be desired. The GTO no longer had an Endura nose. Instead, a massive 5mph impact-resistant bumper fixed prominently in front of twin blacked-out rectangular grilles with a GTO nameplate in the left-hand grille. The parking lamps were placed in the lower bumper, separated by a large air inlet. Large single headlamps were separated by the grilles and a V-shaped nose. That V-shape was picked up on the hood, and twin NACA-style scoops placed back on the hood were nonfunctional unless the scoop cover was unbolted.

Two body styles were offered, the base Le Mans coupe with fixed rear quarter window or the Le Mans sport coupe, which featured a louvered or "Colonnade" rear quarter window treatment. Pontoon-like fender bulges appeared at the front and rear. The rear was distinguished by a one-piece chrome bumper that split the taillamp assembly from a lower valance that rolled under. The taillamps were horizontal and contained the backup lenses in the center. A GTO nameplate decal was located above the right-hand lamp. The name Pontiac was placed between the lamps. The long sloping back window flowed into the rear deck, which ended steeply at the decklid.

The interior was offered in four levels of trim. On Le Mans coupe models, a cloth and Morrokide split bench seat was standard, with an optional all Morrokide bench seat. Stepping up to the Le Mans sport interior, an all-Morrokide notchback bench seat with folding center armrest was standard. The top interior choice was the bucket seat interior, which featured all-Morrokide upholstery and integrated headrests. The door and quarter panels also received special features at this level of trim, including GTO nameplates above the armrests.

The instrument panel featured two large pods on either side of the steering column and one smaller pod above it. Flanking the pods was an air vent and the heater/air conditioning controls. Below them was the switch and control panel that reached from one end of the housing to the other and encompassed the radio. Two Rally Gauge clusters were offered optionally in 1973 that placed either the clock or tachometer in the left-hand pod, the speedometer in the right, and gauges for fuel, oil pressure, and water temperature in the center pod. Three steering wheels were offered: the standard two-spoke Deluxe wheel, the three-spoke Custom Cushion, and the three-spoke Custom Sports.

The three-spoke Custom Cushion steering wheel was optional in 1973. The three-pod instrument panel could be equipped with the optional Rally Gauge cluster. A wood grained facing covered the lower switch and control panel.

1973 GTO Exterior Colors and Codes

Color	Number Code	Letter Code
Cameo Ivory	11	C
Porcelain Blue	24	D
Admiralty Blue	29	E
Regatta Blue	26	F
Desert Sand	56	H
Golden Olive	46	J
Verdant Green	42	K
Slate Green	44	L
Brewster Green	48	M
Florentine Red	74	S
Ascot Silver	64	V
Valencia Gold	60	Y
Burma Brown	68	Z
Mesa Tan	?	?
Burnished Umber	?	?

Cordova Top Colors and Codes

Color	Code
White	1
Black	2
Beige	3
Chamois	4
Green	5
Dark Burgundy	6
Blue	7

1973 GTO Stripe Colors
Bright Blue/Light Blue/Black
Dark Brown/Orange/Cream/Yellow
Lime Green/Red/Black

GTO Decal Colors
Black, White, or Red

Mechanically, there was nothing new for 1973. The suspension and brakes were virtually unchanged from 1972, but the engine lineup lacked any real muscle. Standard was the 400ci engine, rated at 230hp. The only step up was to the 250hp 455, but it was offered only with automatic transmission, and the hottest rear in the book was a 3.23:1.

The public refused to accept the 1973 GTO, and sales fell to 4,806, 1,000 units less than the much more powerful and attractive 1972 GTO.

If the 1973 was a shock to performance fans, the 1974 GTO made them nearly apoplectic. Like an unwanted relative, the GTO had been shuffled off to the compact-sized Ventura lineup as an option, and its once mighty heart reduced to 350ci.

In fairness to Pontiac's marketing department, a trend had developed in the early sev-

Only two engines were offered in 1973, the 400 and 455. The Mallory ignition component and chrome valve cover are incorrect.

enties that favored smaller high-performance cars like Plymouth's 340 Duster. These cars outflanked the stiff insurance surcharges, and Pontiac earnestly believed they could breath new life into the GTO by shifting its position into the compact performance market.

The GTO was offered as an option on either the Ventura or Ventura Custom notchback or hatchback. The notchback had a standard rear deck with trunk, while the hatchback opened to allow additional storage room by folding down the rear seat. The notchback was purchased by 5,335 buyers, while 1,723 customers bought the hatchback.

Both models featured recessed grilles with the parking lamps mounted within and trimmed by Argent Silver surrounds. The

1973 Interior Colors and Codes

Cloth & Vinyl Bench Seat Interior
(Standard) For The Two-Door Hardtop

Color	Code
Green	264
Beige	265

Morrokide Bench Seat Interior
(Standard) For Two-Door Sport Coupe

Color	Code
Blue	251
White	252
Saddle	253
Black	556
Burgundy	257

Morrokide Bench Seat Interior
(Optional) For Two-Door Hardtop

Color	Code
Blue	271
White	272
Saddle	273
Black	276

Morrokide Bucket Seat Interior
(Optional) For Two-Door Sport Coupe

Color	Code
Blue	251
White	252
Saddle	253
Black	556
Burgundy	257
Chamois	258

Assembly Plant Codes For 1973

Code	Plant
P	Pontiac
Z	Fremont
R	Arlington
G	Framingham
B	Baltimore
A	Atlanta

grilles were split by the traditional nose with a Pontiac crest in the center. The massive bumper wrapped around the sides to protect the edges of the fenders and featured optional twin bumperettes framing the front license plate and air inlets on either side. A flexible "closeout" panel covered the gap between the body and the bumper. The single headlamps were trimmed with bright bezels. Above the right-hand grille was a tricolored GTO nameplate decal. The hood is "V"ed, meeting at the point of the nose. It was cut out to accept a

The 1974 GTO option was shifted to the Ventura or Ventura Custom platform and could be ordered with a notchback or hatchback rear. The engine displacement badge below the front marker lamp shown on this preproduction photograph was dropped from production models.

"shaker" hood scoop like the Trans Am, and like the Trans Am, the scoop's inlet faced the cowl. Under full acceleration, a door on the scoop would open, allowing cold air into the Quadra-Jet four-barrel carburetor.

The flanks were clean with bright moldings around the windows. A tricolored GTO nameplate decal appeared on the front fenders behind the wheel opening. On Ventura Custom models, bright rocker panels moldings were used and a "Custom" script appeared on the C-pillar next to the Pontiac crest. An optional vinyl slash stripe ran the length of the car.

The twin taillamps were stacked and incorporated the backup lamps. The rear license plate was recessed between the lamps. On the left rear of the decklid was either a Pontiac nameplate or, on hatchback models, a "Hatchback by Pontiac" emblem. A GTO decal appeared over the right-hand taillamp on the decklid.

The 1974 GTO had a variety of interior combinations. The base Ventura interior started with a bench seat covered in plaid cloth. Next step was an all-Morrokide split bench seat. The top Ventura interior featured front bucket seats. This series of seat configurations was similar in the Ventura Custom, however a plethora of seat and appointment combinations were available. The only color not offered for the bucket seats was black.

1974 GTO Production Figures

Body Style	Production		Engine	Trans
Hatchback	687		350-4bbl	Manual
Hatchback	1,036		350-4bbl	Auto
Total Hatchback	1,723			
Coupe	2,487		350-4bbl	Manual
Coupe	2,848		350-4bbl	Auto
Total Coupe	5,335			
Total Production	7,058			

1974 GTO Engine Codes

Description	Letter ID	UPC
350-4bbl w/Manual Trans	WP	L76
350-4bbl w/Hydra-Matic	YP	L76
350-4bbl w/Hydra-Matic*	ZP	L76
350-4bbl w/Hydra-Matic	YS	L76

All 1974 GTOs were equipped with a 350ci V-8, rated at 200hp at 4400rpm. All had a 7.62:1 compression ratio. All were 4bbl-equipped cars.

* This denotes California use only. Manual transmissions were not available for use in GTOs sold in California in 1974. 1974 GTOs sold in California were equipped with M38 transmissions (Hydra-matic) and a 3:08:1 rear axle.

1974 GTO Transmission and Axle Codes

Description	Letter ID	UPC
Three-Speed Manual Trans	TN	M15
Four-Speed Manual Trans	WC	M20
Hydra-Matic (Auto)	MA	M38
Hydra-Matic H.D.	ME	M38

1974 GTO Axle Codes

Non Safe-T-Track	Safe-T-Track	Ratio
JA	JM	2.73:1
JB	JN	3.08:1

1974 GTO Exterior Colors and Codes

Color	Number Code	Letter Code
Cameo White	11	C
Admiralty Blue	29	E
Regatta Blue	26	F
Carmel Beige	50	G
Denver Gold	53	H
Limefire Green	46	J
Gulfmist Aqua	36	K
Fernmist Green	40	M
Pinemist Green	49	N
Buccaneer Red	75	R
Honduras Maroon	74	S
Sunstorm Yellow	51	T
Ascot Silver	64	V
Fire Coral Bronze	66	W
Colonial Gold	55	Y
Crestwood Brown	59	Z

Cordova Top Colors and Codes

Color	Code
White	1
Black	2
Beige	3
Russet	4
Green	5
Burgundy	6
Blue	7
Brown	8
Saddle	9
Taupe	0

Stripe & Decal Colors Offered

Red/White/Blue Chrome/Black
Light Orange/Dark Orange
Light Green/Dark Green or White

A large, tricolored nameplate decal was placed on the front fender, directly behind the wheel opening.

Interior Trim Colors and Codes

Ventura Standard Interior
Cloth and Morrokide

Black/White/Red	502
Black/White/Green	523

Morrokide-Standard

Saddle/Orange	503
Black/White/Red	555
Green/Yellow	574
Black/White/Red*	502
Black/White/Red**	552

* Plaid w/Red Appointments.
** With Red Appointments.

Cloth & Morrokide Split Bench Seat
Ventura Custom

Black	522
Green	564

Available All Morrokide Split Bench Seat

White	542
Saddle	563
Green	584
Black*	522
Green*	584
White***	544

* Black Trim, White Seats.
** Green Trim, White Seats.
*** White w/Red or Green Appointments.

Optional Bucket Seats Colors and Codes

White	262
Saddle	565
Green	567
Red	568
Green*	567
Red**	568
White***	262

* White Seats, Green Trim.
** White Seats, Red Trim.
*** White Trim, Red Appointments.

White	542
Red	550
Saddle	563
Green	584
Red*	550
Green**	584
White***	542

* Red Trim, White Seats.
** Green Trim, White Seats.
*** White Trim, Green/Red Appointments.

Assembly Plant Codes for 1974

Code	Plant
L	Van Nuys
W	Willow Run

Another GTO nameplate decal appeared on the rear deck, just above the twin taillamps. Notice the "close-out" panel fitted between the bumper and the body.

The top GTO interior featured bucket seats. The standard steering wheel was the two-spoke Deluxe model, with horn buttons on each spoke. Compared to GTOs of the past, the base 1974 interior was stark. Notice the placement of the four-speed shifter on the tunnel without console.

The instrument panel consisted of a large horizontal speedometer with fuel gauge to the left and vertically positioned heater control panel to the right, surrounded by a pebble-grained finish. A panel in the lower portion of the panel, flanking the steering column, contained light and wiper controls on the left and the radio on the right. A buyer who ordered the optional bucket seat interior could also order a floor console that placed a tachometer in the instrument panel and moved the fuel gauge to the console, along with an oil pressure gauge, battery gauge, and water temperature gauge.

The standard steering wheel was the twin-spoke Deluxe wheel with horn buttons in each spoke, followed by the Custom Cushion three-spoke and the three-spoke Custom Sport. While a tilt column was offered, cruise control was not.

Since the Ventura was a unit-bodied car, its rear suspension pieces attached directly to the body, while the front used a subframe like

Only one engine was offered in 1974, the 200hp 350ci with a shaker air cleaner that poked through the hood. Under full acceleration, a flap would open to feed cold air into the carburetor.

the Nova and Camaro/Firebird to attach the engine and front suspension members. Around back, multileaf springs suspended the Salisbury axle. The GTO came standard with a small diameter rear antisway bar. In front, unequal length control arms were used with coil springs and larger antisway bar. An RTS (Radial Tuned Suspension) was offered in 1974. The RTS featured different shock and spring rates for use with the FR78x14 radial tires. The standard GTO tire size was E70x14 on Rally II wheels.

The only engine offered in 1975 was a 350ci powerplant rated at 200hp, while three transmission options were available: a three-speed manual, four-speed manual, and the M38 automatic. The lowest rear gear ratio was 3.08:1.

What to Look Out For

Since the 1973 GTO was composite construction, it suffers the usual troubles that plague separate body/frame cars. Frame rot at the rear axle kickup is common. Body rust out around the rear window is common on all GM cars of this era, and it's not unusual to find lower quarter panels riddled with rust out on the 1973s. The massive doors have a tendency to sag, and the bottoms can be severely rusted. Hoods have a tendency to bend at the hinges. Water leakage around the front windows is also a problem. The Morrokide interiors are virtually indestructible, but the dash pads are prone to fading and cracking. Worn and faded carpets are also quite common.

The 1974 GTO is another story altogether. Trunkpan rust is common on hatchback models, and both body styles can have severe floorpan rust. The leaf springs usually sag on hatchbacks, and leaky steering boxes are not unusual. Rust around the taillamps can occur from poor weathersealing, and front fender rust is not unusual. The interiors did not last as well as other GTOs.

Best Buys

Both the 1973 and 1974 GTOs are hard to recommend as collectibles. They were not accepted by enthusiasts in their time, and that stigma still plagues them today. The few 1973 GTOs that were equipped with Ram Air carry about 10 percent more value then non-Ram-Air-equipped models. Finding parts for these two years is quite difficult. Few reproduction parts exist, and they share almost nothing with earlier models. Neither the 1973 or 1974 are recommended investments or are considered collectibles, although in polls taken by the GTO Association of America, the 1974 GTO fared slightly better in popularity then the 1973.

Both cars are fun drivers, however. The 1974 is better on gas but does not have as much interior room for larger drivers as does the 1973. For the time being, their status among GTO collectors is strictly second class, and that probably won't change for a long time to come.

Sources

Ames Performance Engineering
Bonny Road
Marlborough, NH 03455
603-876-4514
Reproduction and NOS parts and accessories

Performance Years GTOs
279 Stahl Road
Harleysville, PA 19434
215-256-GOAT
Reproduction and NOS parts and accessories

Purely PMD
500 Carmony NE
Albuquerque, NM 87107
505-344-3513
Engine rebuilding, restoration, NOS and reproduction parts

Just Dashes
5941 Lemona Ave
Van Nuys, CA 91411
1-800-247-3274
Dash pad restoration

Dennis Kirban GTOs
1482 Sugar Bottom Road
Furlong, PA 18925
215-348-8671
Reproduction and NOS parts and accessories

The Paddock
221 W. Main Street
Box 30
Knightstown, IN 46148
1-800-428-4319
Reproduction and NOS parts and accessories

Original Parts Group
17842 Gothard St.
Huntington Beach, CA 92647
714-841-5363
Reproduction and NOS parts and accessories

Year One
4559 Granite Drive
Tucker, GA 33669
404-493-6568
Reproduction and NOS parts and accessories

GTO Association of America
5829 Stroebel Road
Saginaw, MI 48609

Coker Tire
1317 Chestnut St
PO Box 72554
Chattanooga, TN 37407
1-800-999-TYRE
Reproduction performance tires

Goat Farm
85 N. 27th Street
San Jose, CA 95116
408-295-7611
New and used GTO parts

H-O Racing
PO Box 429 G1
Hawthorne, CA 90250
213-973-7078
Specialists in suspension and brake
upgrades

Just Suspensions
PO Box 167
Towaco, NJ
201-335-0547
Complete line of suspension components

A&M Soffseal
104 May Drive
Harrison, OH 45030
1-800-426-0902
Complete line of weatherstripping

Custom Mold Dynamics
5161 Wolfpen-Pleasant Hill Road
Milford, OH 45150
513-831-1472
Complete line of exterior trim and emblems

Metro Molded Parts
11610 Jay Street
Minneapolis, MN 55433
612-757-0310
Complete line of rubber parts

Classic Reproductions
5315 Meeker Road
Greensville, OH 45331
513-548-9839
Reproduction sheet metal replacement
parts

Restoration Battery
3335 Robinet Drive
Cincinnati, OH 45238
513-451-1038
Original style reproduction GM Delco
batteries

Jim Osborn Reproductions
101 Ridgecrest Drive
Lawrenceville, GA 30245
912-962-7556
Reproduction window stickers and decals

Tygersoft Programs
PO Box 1222
Vernal, UT 84078
801-789-4867
GTO database computer program

CPI Value Guide
PO Box 3190
Laurel, MD 20709
1-800-972-5312
Quarterly collector cars value guide

Index